U.S. Mint

Miscellaneous Letters Received from 1897 to 1903

Vol. 10

U.S. Mint

Miscellaneous Letters Received from 1897 to 1903
Vol. 10

ISBN/EAN: 9783337817183

Printed in Europe, USA, Canada, Australia, Japan

Cover: Foto ©Suzi / pixelio.de

More available books at **www.hansebooks.com**

RG 104, 8KRA-104-84-042
Box 5, Volume X

Miscellaneous Letters Received, 1897-1903. Letters Received Relating to the Construction of the New Denver Mint, 1897-1906.

DENVER NEW MINT.

Inclosure 1282.

IN REPLYING, QUOTE UPPER INITIAL, RIGHT HAND CORNER

TREASURY DEPARTMENT

WASHINGTON Feb.9,1904.

Superintendent of Construction,
New Mint Building,
Denver,Colorado.

Sir:

I inclose herewith, for your information and the files of your office, a copy of Department letter of even date, accepting the proposal of James A.McGonigle, in amount two hundred and fifteen dollars ($215.00), as an addition to his contract for the completion of the building in your charge, for placing hatchway and two wall boxes in engine room in basement; and you are hereby authorized to certify and issue vouchers for the work, as required by the terms of the contract and the printed "Instructions to Superintendents", payment of which vouchers the Disbursing Agent has been authorized to make from the appropriation for Mint Building, Denver,Colorado.

Respectfully,

J K Taylor
Supervising Architect.

JSS

Mr. James A. McGonigle,
New Mint Building,
Denver, Colorado.

Sir:

In view of the statement and recommendation contained in letter of December 5,1903 from the Superintendent of Construction of the New Mint Building, Denver, Colorado, and in accordance with the approval of this Department, your proposal, dated December 3,1903, in amount two hundred and fifteen dollars ($215.00), is hereby accepted, as an addition to your contract dated August 25, 1902 for the completion of the building, for placing hatchway and two wall boxes in engine room in basement, where indicated on drawings 81-A and 248, a public exigency requiring the changes in the work.

It is understood and agreed that this acceptance is not to affect the time for the completion of the work as required by the terms of your contract; that the same is without prejudice to any and all rights of the United States thereunder; and without prejudice, also, to any and all rights of the United States against the sureties on the bond executed for the faithful fulfillment of the contract.

Please acknowledge the receipt of this letter.

Respectfully,

Assistant Secretary.

T.
C.J.P.
JM

(PRINTED HEADING).

Philadelphia, February 10,1904.

Mr.Lee Ullery,

Supt.Construction,New Mint Building,

Denver, Colorado.

Sir:-

Complying with the request contained in your letter of the 13th ultimo,we have to state that we will change the ash hoist at the Mint Building,Denver, Colorado, so that it will discharge toward the south instead of to the west, as at present, make the necessary changes in the concrete foundation,iron work,etc., for the sum of ONE HUNDRED AND FIFTY DOLLARS ($150.00).

We have also to state that we will move said ash hoist four feet to the west of its present location and make necessary changes in foundation,pit,etc., the hoist to discharge towards the west,as at present, for the sum of EIGHTY DOLLARS($80.00).

Respectfully,

(Signed) S.Faith & Co.,
Metzger.

[illegible] & Co.

[illegible]

[illegible]

[illegible]

[illegible]

We [illegible] for time [illegible]

[illegible]

[illegible]

[illegible]

[illegible]

Awaiting [illegible]

Yours [illegible]

[illegible]

[illegible]

[illegible]

DENVER NEW MINT.

Inclosure 1503,

TREASURY DEPARTMENT

4

WASHINGTON Feb.13,1904.

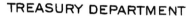

Superintendent of Construction,
New Mint Building,
Denver,Colorado.

Sir:

I inclose herewith, for your information and the files of your office, a copy of Department letter of even date,accepting the proposal of S.Faith & Company, in amount sixty-seven dollars ($67.00), as an addition to their contract for the mechanical equipment of the building in your charge, to substitute rubber-covered,in place of slow-burning,weatherproof wire, in and on boiler room ceiling;and you are hereby authorized to certify and issue vouchers for the work, as required by the terms of the contract and the printed "Instructions to Superintendents",payment of which vouchers the Disbursing Agent has been authorized to make from the appropriation for Mint Building,Denver,Colorado.

You will note the rejection of the said company's proposal, in amount two hundred and forty-seven dollars ($247.00), for covering feeder conduits in boiler room with metal lath and plaster; and you are directed to obtain from the contractor for the completion of the building a proposal for this work,and to forward the same to this Office with your definite recommendation.

Respectfully,

Acting Supervising Architect.

JSS

DENVER NEW MINT.

Feb. 12, 1894.

Messrs. S. Waite & Co.,
[illegible] Pennsylvania Avenue,
Philadelphia, Pa.

Gentlemen:

In view of the statement and recommendation contained in letter of the 3d instant, from the Superintendent of Construction of the new Mint building, Denver, Colorado, your proposal, dated the 30th ultimo, in amount sixty-seven dollars ($67.00), is hereby accepted, as an addition to your contract dated August 1, 1893 for the mechanical equipment of the said building, to substitute rubber-covered, in place of fire-burning, weather-proof wire, in and on boiler room ceiling, a public exigency requiring this change in the work.

It is understood and agreed that this acceptance is not to affect the time for the completion of the work as required by the terms of your contract; that the same is without prejudice to any and all rights of the United States thereunder, and without prejudice, also, to any and all rights of the United States against the sureties on the bond executed for the faithful fulfillment of the contract.

Your proposal, in amount two hundred and forty-seven dollars ($247.00), for covering feeder conduits in boiler room ceiling with metal lath and plaster, is rejected, the same being deemed excessive.

Please acknowledge the receipt of this letter.

Respectfully,

Acting Secretary.

F.
J.O.P.

DENVER NEW MINT.

OFFICE OF SUPERVISING ARCHITECT

IN REPLYING, QUOTE UPPER INITIAL, RIGHT HAND CORNER

Inclosure 1281.

TREASURY DEPARTMENT

WASHINGTON Feb.9,1904.

Superintendent of Construction,
New Mint Building,
Denver, Colo.

Sir:

I inclose herewith, for your information and the files of your office, a copy of Department letter of even date, accepting the proposal of James A. McGonigle, in amount one hundred dollars ($100), as an addition to his contract for the completion of the building in your charge, for certain furring in the basement corridor; and you are hereby authorized to certify and issue vouchers for the work, as required by the terms of the contract and the printed "Instructions to Superintendents", payment of which vouchers the Disbursing Agent has been authorized to make from the appropriation for Mint Building, Denver, Colorado.

JWB

Respectfully,

J K Taylor
Supervising Architect.

JSS

Mr. James A. McGonigle,
New Mint Building,
Denver, Colorado.

Sir:

In view of the statement and recommendation contained in letter of the 28th ultimo, from the Superintendent of Construction of the New Mint Building, Denver, Colorado, and in accordance with the approval of this Department, your proposal, dated the 26th ultimo, in amount one hundred dollars ($100.00), is hereby accepted, as an addition to your contract dated August 25, 1902, for the completion of the building, a public exigency requiring the immediate performance of the work, to do certain furring in the basement corridor, as stated.

It is understood and agreed that this acceptance is not to affect the time for the completion of the work as required by the terms of your contract; that the same is without prejudice to any and all rights of the United States thereunder; and without prejudice, also, to any and all rights of the United States against the sureties on the bond executed for the faithful fulfillment of the contract.

Please acknowledge the receipt of this letter.

Respectfully,

Assistant Secretary.

T.

Superintendent of Construction,
New Mint Building,
Denver, Colorado.

[illegible] 27.

[illegible] for your information
your office, a copy of Department letter o
the proposal of S. Faith & Co., in amount o
two dollars ($124.00), as an addition to t
mechanical equipment of the building in yo
the run of the 5" cast iron soil and the
pipes at the rear of the building; and you
to certify and issue vouchers for the work
terms of the contract and the printed "Ins
intendents", payment of which vouchers the
been authorized to make from the appropria
[illegible]

FAB

Respectfully,

JCS

[illegible]
Supe[illegible]

S. Smith & Co.,
[illegible] Pennsylvania Avenue,
Philadelphia, Pa.

Feb. 10, 1904.

Gentlemen:-

In view of the statement and recommendation contained in letter of the 30th ultimo, from the Superintendent of Construction of the new Mint Building, Denver, Colorado, and in accordance with the approval of this Department, your proposal, dated January 23, 1904, in amount one hundred and thirty-two dollars ($132.00), is hereby accepted, as an addition to your contract dated August 9, 1903 for the mechanical equipment of the said building, to change the run of the 8" cast iron soil and the 8" terra cotta waste pipes at rear of building, in accordance with the terms of your proposal, and to the satisfaction of the Superintendent, a public exigency requiring the changes in the work, on account of the City sewer being higher than reported by the City Engineer at the time the work was laid out.

It is understood and agreed that this acceptance is not to affect the time for the completion of the work as required by the terms of your contract, that the same is without prejudice to any and all rights of the United States thereunder; and without prejudice, also, to any and all rights of the United States against the sureties on the bond executed for the faithful fulfillment of the contract.

Please acknowledge the receipt of this letter.

Respectfully,

Assistant Secretary.

[illegible]

DENVER, NEW MINT.
SBP

OFFICE OF SUPERVISING ARCHITECT

IN REPLYING, QUOTE UPPER INITIAL, RIGHT HAND CORNER.

7
HSW
O-1

TREASURY DEPARTMENT

WASHINGTON February 12, 1904.

Superintendent of Construction,

U. S. Mint (new),

Denver, Colorado.

Sir:

In reply to your letter of the 6th instant, relative to the status of Inspector Saville, recently detailed to your building, you are advised that the Inspector is to assist you in giving proper supervision and inspection of the work incident to installation of the plumbing, heating and ventilating, hoisting, and lighting systems, the same as Inspector Thompson formerly at the building, and that his presence there does not in any way relieve you from the care and responsibility for that work. As previously advised, the Inspector is to submit to this Office, through you, weekly reports on the character of workmanship and material supplied, and progress made in the work. These reports, if they meet with your approval, should be checked by you before transmission to this Office. Should they be at any time and in any manner at variance with your judgment, you should withhold approval of same, submitting instead separate reports in the premises, stating specifically wherein the Inspector's statements or recommendations are not concurred in; the Inspector's reports to be forwarded in such cases without your check.

Respectfully,

Supervising Architect.

DENVER, NEW MINT.

OFFICE OF SUPERVISING ARCHITECT

IN REPLYING, QUOTE UPPER INITIAL RIGHT HAND CORNER.

TREASURY DEPARTMENT 8 JP.

WASHINGTON Feb. 17, 1904.

FORWARDING.

Superintendent of Construction,
New Mint Building,
Denver, Colorado.

Sir:-

I have to acknowledge receipt of your letter of the 12th instant, relative to copy of drawings Nos. 31-A and 248, and you are advised that a copy of each of these drawings is forwarded herewith, under separate cover.

Respectfully,

J. K. Taylor
Supervising Architect.

kcm

(PRINTED HEADING).

Leavenworth, Kansas, February 17, 1904.

Mr. Lee Ullery,

Supt. Mint Building,

Denver, Colorado.

Dear Sir:-

At your request I submit the following bid:

I will furnish material and labor and complete Storage Cellar at Mint Building, Denver, Colorado, according to plans for $7,885.oo. According to plan brick arch construction, $8,285.oo.

Yours truly,

(Signed) James A. McGonigle.

THE RICHARDS & CONOVER HARDWARE COMPANY.

(PRINTED HEADING).

Kansas City, Mo., February 12,1904.

Mr. James A. McGonigle,

Denver, Colorado.

Dear Sir:-

The makers of the hardware for the Denver Mint Building state positively that it will be necessary for them to have the information regarding where the knobs for the bolts on the double doors will be placed, that is, the heights from the floor, as it is necessary to have this information in order to make the goods up. We also again call your attention to the fact that the system of master keys must be known by the makers before the locks can be made. The delay in getting this information will certainly delay the goods longer than you desire.

Yours truly,

(Signed) W.B. Richards.

DENVER, NEW MINT.

OFFICE OF SUPERVISING ARCHITECT

IN REPLYING, QUOTE UPPER INITIAL RIGHT HAND CORNER

11

TREASURY DEPARTMENT

WASHINGTON Feb. 16, 1904.

Superin tendent of Construction,
New Mint Building,
Denver, Colorado.

Sir:-

I have to acknowledge receipt of your letter of the 12th instant, relative to the placing of T irons in certain basement window sash at the building in your charge, and you are directed to obtain a proposal in the nature of a deduction for omitting these irons and forward it to this Office with your definite recommendation, upon receipt of which prompt action will be taken.

Respectfully,

Supervising Architect.

KCH

DENVER, NEW MINT.
SBP

OFFICE OF SUPERVISING ARCHITECT

IN REPLYING, QUOTE UPPER INITIAL, RIGHT HAND CORNER.

12

TREASURY DEPARTMENT

WASHINGTON February 17, 1904.

(INCLOSURE 518)
(FORWARDING)

Superintendent of Construction,

United States Mint (new),

Denver, Colorado.

Sir:

There is enclosed herewith, for your information and files, copy of Office letter this day addressed to S. Faith & Co., contractors for the mechanical equipment of the building for which you are Superintendent of Construction, transmitting one copy each of drawings E. W. 266, E. W. 267, and E. W. 268, showing modified details of back connections of switchboard panels, superseding drawings E. W. 256, E. W. 257, and E. W. 260, respectively, as per Department letter addressed to them under date of the 5th instant, copy of which was duly forwarded to you.

A set of the new drawings is being forwarded to you under separate cover.

Respectfully,

Supervising Architect.

DENVER, NEW MINT.
SBF

TREASURY DEPARTMENT

February 17, 1904.

(FORWARDING)

Messrs. H. Faith & Co.,

2627-29 Pennsylvania Avenue,

Philadelphia, Pennsylvania.

Gentlemen:

As per Department letter addressed to you under date of the 5th instant, there are being forwarded to you under separate cover one copy each of drawings E. W. 266, E. W. 267, and E. W. 268, showing modified details of back connections of switchboard panels, in connection with your contract for the mechanical equipment of the United States Mint (new) at Denver, Colorado, said drawings superseding drawings E. W. 256, E. W. 257 and E. W. 260, respectively.

Respectfully,

(Signed) J. K. Taylor

Supervising Architect.

...made the finish ... fastened
direct ... to wall ...
... tacked ...
... can be ... nailing casing
but ... will ... one on a ...
if preferred

Planing Mill Co.

[illegible]

[illegible]

566

[illegible]

[illegible]

[illegible]

[illegible]

[illegible]

[illegible]

[illegible]

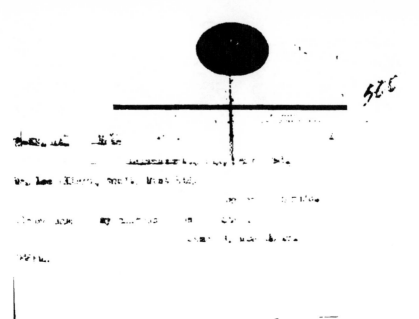

DENVER, NEW MINT.

Feb. 24, 1904.

Mr. James A. McGonigle,
New Mint Building,
Denver, Colorado.

Sir:-

I have to acknowledge receipt of your letter of the 17th instant, relative to samples of hardware which you state that you submitted for approval in connection with your contract for the completion of the new mint building at Denver, Colorado, and you are advised that as the list of hardware mentioned appears to cover that previously submitted by you, and upon which action has been taken on September 24, 1903 and November 11, 1903, it is not understood why they should be resubmitted.

Respectfully,

Supervising Architect.

RCW

DENVER NEW MINT.

Enclosure 681.

Superintendent of Construction,
New Mint,
Denver Colorado.

Sir:

Enclosed find copy of a report dated the [illegible] [illegible] as the result of an examination at the shops, of the [illegible] finish work for the building under your charge.

The report will explain itself, and noting the sta[illegible] therein as to the dividing of certain members, your atte[illegible] is called to the provisions of the specification which r[illegible] that "all workmanship to be of the best known to the [illegible] trades."

Respectfully,

Supervising Architect.

OFFICE OF

SUPERINTENDENT OF Construction,

U. S. Buildings, La. Purchase Exposition,

St. Louis, Mo., February 15, 1904.

The Supervising Architect,

Treasury Department,

Washington, D. C.

Sir:

In compliance with the instructions contained in your letter (S.) dated the 13th ultimo, I have to report that a visit was recently made to the Charles A. Olcott Planing Mill Company's establishment, where an examination was made of certain interior finish being prepared under a contract with James A. McGonigle for construction of the New Mint Building at Denver, Colorado.

The work examined consisted of certain interior finish for the first, second and attic storys, and was found to be fairly satisfactory. The method of dividing certain members was not in all cases such as I should prefer, though from the information at hand it appears that permission has been given the mill to do this work as judgment might dictate. The sketch below will illustrate one point observed. In this connection it may be stated that I am of the opinion much better results would obtain if the division of these parts were shown on the full size details, or otherwise require the contractor to submit for approval such jointing as he may desire to use.

The mill reports that certain of the doors will be ready for examination in about ten days or two weeks.

Respectfully,
(Signed) G. B. Strickler.
Superintendent.

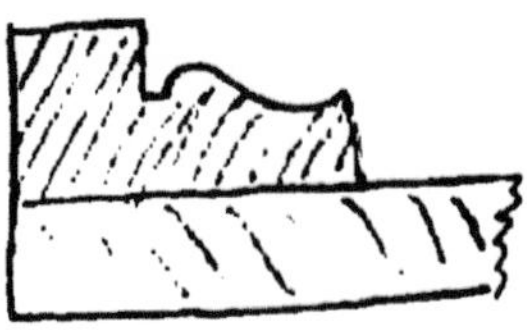

executed

as writer would suggest

CHEYENNE.

OFFICE OF SUPERVISING ARCHITECT

IN REPLYING QUOTE UPPER INITIAL RIGHT HAND CORNER

(ENCLOSURE #724)

18

TREASURY DEPARTMENT FBW

WASHINGTON February 25,1904.

The Superintendent of Construction,

U.S. Mint Building,

Denver,Colorado.

Sir:

For your information and guidance in the inspection of certain ornamental iron work to be supplied in connection with the U.S. Public Building at Cheyenne,Wyoming,there is enclosed herewith one print each of contractor's shop drawings Nos.128 and 129.

Respectfully,

Supervising Architect.

B.

(PRINTED HEADING).

Philadelphia, February 26,1904.

Mr.Lee Ullery,

Supt.Construction U.S.Mint(New),

Denver, Colorado.

Dear Sir:-

Replying to your inquiry of February 8th,asking for price for installing flush instruments on switchboard for the U.S.Mint, Denver,Colorado, would advise you that we propose to install the following instruments:

2 recording voltmeters
2 " ammeters,
1 total light "
1 " power "
3 general panel "
2 ground detectors,

substituting flush type of instruments in lieu of the regular patterns as specified for the sum of SEVEN HUNDRED AND TWENTY FIVE DOLLARS ($725.oo).

Relative to the above, we herewith give you a quotation from a letter received from the manufacturer.

"We note that you state that you think your customer will be obliged to return these to have them changed for flush mounting. We have never made any of the ammeters of this range in this way,and do not know just how we can arrange to do so without making an entirely different design, and consequently would not be able to make a price at this time on such. While we can make the voltmeters in this style,we have not as yet any regular design for same also. We would prefer not to cut such large holes in the panels as it will greatly weaken them".

Awaiting your decision as to the above estimate,we remain

Yours respectfully,

(Signed) S.Faith & Co.,

DENVER, NEW MINT

INCLOSURE #1793 TREASURY DEPARTMENT 41

WASHINGTON Feb.27,1904.

Superintendent of Construction,
New Mint Building,
Denver, Colorado.

Sir:

I have to acknowledge receipt of your letter of the 16th instant relative to partition in Weigh Clerk's room, in the building under your charge, indicated on drawing #125, and there is inclosed herewith a drawing showing certain changes from the arrangement required by the contract, and you are directed to obtain a proposal based thereon, and forward it to this Office, as soon as possible, with your definite recommendation.

Respectfully,

J K Taylor
Supervising Architect.

HM

DENVER, NEW MINT.

OFFICE OF SUPERVISING ARCHITECT

IN REPLYING, QUOTE UPPER INITIAL, RIGHT HAND CORNER.

22

TREASURY DEPARTMENT

WASHINGTON Feb. 29, 1904.

Superintendent of Construction,
New Mint Building,
Denver, Colo.

Sir:-

I have to acknowledge receipt of your letter of the 20th instant, relative to "Live steam to gas generator" in fuel gas generating room at the building in your charge, and you are advised that the live steam pipe to new gas generator room should be run at ceiling of boiler room, ash vault, and well room, just through the wall of the gas generator room, in such a place across well room as will clear the hatch, or space reserved for same. The new line should be of 2" pipe with 1 1/4" outlet about the middle of well room, and with end in generator room capped; and you are directed to secure from the contractor a proposal for the above work and a separate proposal for the omission of the live steam pipe in the trench to gas generator room, as called for on drawing H-80, and forward such proposals to this Office with your definite recommendation, upon receipt of which prompt action will be taken.

Respectfully,

Supervising Architect.

KCH

DENVER MINT (NEW):

MGD

OFFICE OF SUPERVISING ARCHITECT

IN REPLYING QUOTE UPPER INITIAL, RIGHT HAND CORNER

20

TREASURY DEPARTMENT FBW

WASHINGTON February 29,1904.

The Superintendent of Construction,

U. S. Mint (New),

Denver, Col.

Sir:

Replying to your letter of the 25th instant, relative to doors for closet enclosures in the building for which you are Superintendent, you are advised that said doors in toilet rooms 3 and 4 should be provided with vertical center stiles, same as shown for doors of other toilet rooms, making these four-panel doors.

Respectfully,

J K Taylor

Supervising Architect.

DENVER, NEW MINT.

OFFICE OF SUPERVISING ARCHITECT

IN REPLYING QUOTE UPPER INITIAL, RIGHT HAND CORNER.

24

TREASURY DEPARTMENT FBW

WASHINGTON February 29,1904.

FORWARDING.
ENCLOSURE-1583.

FLa

The Superintendent of Construction,

New Mint Building,

Denver, Colorado.

Sir:

There is enclosed herewith for your information and files a copy of office letter this day addressed to The Diebold Safe & Lock Company, and, under separate cover, approved print of drawing No.5400 for certain vault work to be supplied under the contract for the building of which you are the Superintendent of Construction.

Respectfully,

J. K. Taylor
Supervising Architect.

M.

DENVER NEW MINT.

In replying to this letter the initials in upper right hand corner must be referred to.

TREASURY DEPARTMENT,

OFFICE OF THE SUPERVISING ARCHITECT,

Washington, February 29,1904.

The Diebold Safe & Lock Company,

Canton, Ohio.

Gentlemen:

The receipt of your letter of the 24th instant with print in quadruplicate of shop drawing No.5400 for certain vault work to be supplied under your contract in connection with the New Mint Building at Denver, Colorado, is hereby acknowledged, and in reply you are advised that the sealing device as shown thereby has been approved in lieu of that formerly submitted; one copy of the print being herewith returned.

The question of using forged steel for the pressure bar housings will form the subject of a separate communication.

Respectfully,

J. K. TAYLOR,

Supervising Architect.

M.

(PRINTED HEADING).

28

Denver, Colo., March 4th,1904.

Mr.Lee Ullery,

Superintendent of Construction,U.S.Mint

Denver, Colorado.

Dear Sir:-

In view of the fact that an attempt has been made by the parties (who have contract to set vaults E.F.and G in this Mint Building),to have such work done by non-union labor,and further conceding to you your full authority by reason of your office to say who may or may not be employed in this building, yet I most respectfully call your attention to the fact that all workmen employed by the undersigned in the prosecution of his work has and are now Union men who absolutely and immediately one and all refuse to continue work on this building if any non-union men are allowed to work on it in any capacity. Hence,Sir you can readily see that all our work will have to stop if such is allowed,you yourself knowing well the conditions that obtain in this city and we hope we shall not be troubled or interfered with by the use of non-union Mechanics if only for a few days work.

Very respectfully,

(Signed) James A.McGonigle,

by C.Anderson, Foreman.

[illegible] Denver, March 8,

Mr [illegible],

Supt Construction, [illegible] Building

Denver, Colorado

Sir

Referring to the matter of employing one union man on our work on the [illegible] Building, or keeping one union man on each of our [illegible] who are employed [illegible] other [illegible] the building, we still state that we cannot do either and proceed with our work, and as we are doing contract work at various places throughout the country, we cannot afford to have any contest at this time or [illegible] later on time.

Respectfully

DENVER NEW MINT.

OFFICE OF SUPERVISING ARCHITECT

N REPLYING QUOTE UPPER INITIAL RIGHT HAND CORNER

Inclosure 1520.

27

TREASURY DEPARTMENT

WASHINGTON March 1,1904.

Superintendent of Construction,
New Mint Building,
Denver,Colorado.

Sir:

I inclose herewith, for your information and the files of your office, a copy of Department letter of even date,accepting the proposal of S.Faith & Company, in amount eighty dollars ($80.00), as an addition to their contract for the mechanical equipment of the building in your charge, for changing location of ash hoist,etc.;and you are hereby authorized to certify and issue vouchers for the work, as required by the terms of their contract and the printed "Instructions to Superintendents", payment of which vouchers the Disbursing Agent has been authorized to make from the appropriation for Mint Building,Denver,Colorado.

Respectfully,

Supervising Architect.

JSS

March 1,1904.

Messrs S.Faith & Co.,
Care of Superintendent of Construction,New Mint Building,
Denver,Colorado.

Gentlemen:

In view of the statements contained in letter of the 16th ultimo,from the Superintendent of Construction of the new Mint Building,Denver,Colorado, your proposal, of the same date, addressed to him, in amount eighty dollars ($80.00), is hereby accepted, as an addition to your contract dated August 8,1902 for the mechanical equipment of the said building, to move ash hoist four feet to the west of its present location,and make changes in foundation,pit,etc.,in accordance with the terms of your proposal, and to the satisfaction of the Superintendent,a public exigency requiring the changes in the work.

It is understood and agreed that this acceptance is not to affect the time for the completion of the work as required by the terms of your contract;that the same is without prejudice to any and all rights of the United States thereunder;and without prejudice,also, to any and all rights of the United States against the sureties on the bond executed for the faithful fulfillment of the contract.

Please acknowledge the receipt of this letter.

Respectfully,

Assistant Secretary.

R.
J.C.P.

JSS

DENVER, NEW MINT.

OFFICE OF SUPERVISING ARCHITECT

IN REPLYING QUOTE UPPER INITIAL, RIGHT HAND CORNER

28

TREASURY DEPARTMENT

WASHINGTON March 4, 1904.

Superintendent of Construction,
New Mint Building,
Denver, Colorado.

Sir:-

I have to acknowledge receipt of your letter of the 29th ultimo, relative to a copy of letter dated the 24th ultimo, addressed to Mr. James A. McGonigle, relative to hardware samples, and you are advised that further consideration was not given to the samples referred to inasmuch as he submitted a second time all the samples included in the first shipment, upon which action had already been taken.

Respectfully,

Supervising Architect.

KCH

Architect,

Treasury Department,

Washington, D. C.

In answer to your letter of

that we sent statement of Feb. 2

amount of work completed at the

your attention to the manner in

good for us to send our statement

n on the building, as he ignores

o our contract, received far more

ease of bringing it to your atten

to same. We remain,

DENVER. New MINT.

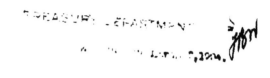

TREASURY DEPARTMENT

[illegible] 7,1904.

Messrs.S.Faith and Company,
No.2429 Pennsylvania avenue,
Philadelphia, Pennsylvania.

Sirs:

Referring to the statements contained in your letter of the 29th ultimo, in relation to the estimate of payments alleged to be due under your contract for the mechanical equipment, &c., at the New Mint, Denver, Colorado, you are advised that payments on account of the work already made would seem to be in accordance with the terms of the contract, based on the value of such work satisfactorily in place complete. Payments due you can only be determined at the building and by the representative of the office in charge of the work at that point.

In the estimate submitted by you under date of the 22nd ultimo, it is noted that certain items are given and valued which the office (basing its belief on the reports on file) does not think are in place complete, and therefore the same cannot be included in any estimates made by the Superintendent as the basis of payments, and unless more satisfactory proof can be submitted by you as an evidence that the Superintendent is unwarranted under the terms of your contract in the estimates made by him, no further action on the part of the office would seem to be necessary.

It is also proper to suggest, in this connection, that better expedition in the supply of your work in place complete will not only avoid delaying the other branches of the work, but will tend to increase the amount of payments due you in accordance with the terms of your agreement.

A copy of your letter and of this reply have this day been transmitted to the Superintendent at the building for his information.

Respectfully,

(Signed) J.K. Taylor

Supervising Architect.

ALA

DENVER MINT (NEW)
SBP

TREASURY DEPARTMENT

WASHINGTON, March [illegible], [illegible]01.

Superintendent of Construction,

U. S. Mint (new),

Denver, Colorado.

Sir:

Referring to your letter of the 15th ultimo, relative to the oil tanks to be installed at the building for which you are Superintendent of Construction, it is desired that you advise this Office when the tanks have been delivered and properly placed in position on their foundations. Filling must not be placed around or on the tanks until after inspection is made of the same as may be desired by the Director of the Mint.

Respectfully,

[illegible] Supervising Architect.

The Supervising Architect,
Treasury Department.

Sir:

Acting on instructions, "S.", dated the 5th ultimo, I visited the shops of the Diebold Safe & Lock Co. on the 8th ultimo to examine into progress of vault work under contract with that Company for the Denver New Mint. A report of the inspection was epitomized in the telegram of that date:-"Progress here good, etc., etc." I arrived in that city again on the 20th, and, after the intervening Sunday and holiday, inspection was continued until evening of the 25th ultimo.

The new material at hand was the steel castings for jamb shields and soft iron castings for thresholds and bridges. All seemed sound. There were extra castings off each pattern and only perfect castings will be used.

Progress on the vestibules had reached the stage of hardening the door plates and beginning the assembling of the operating parts for the four smaller vaults:-all in a first class manner. Active assembling of the accompanying linings was to have been begun on the 29th ultimo. These will be completed before the vestibules. The completion of the vestibules will mark the time for shipping each set and the work is so far advanced that a nearly accurate estimate can be made.

They expect to have the vestibules and linings for vaults E and F set up complete for final shop inspection by the 24th instant and ship same one week later. Those for vaults G and H will follow within 3 weeks. About 40 days will be required for transportation and erection complete in place, all to be finished before June 1st, next. The six vault doors and one closet door for the minor vaults in the building were being finished in paint shops. These will be ready for shipment by the [illegible] instant but will be held until vaults E and F are ready.

As reported under date of July 22 190[illegible], the Diebold Co. have so many large jobs under way that the Denver Mint vaults has to wait for their turn among the orders filed, for floor space, convenient to the proper machinery upon which they could be constructed. That report is pertinent as, while it appears reasonable that all the small vaults [illegible] to completion will be completed in place before the time limit expires, on June 15th, next, they have not been able heretofore to find room for construction of the large Storage vault. All the forgings have been made for the vestibule, the hoop has been hardened, and arrangements made to begin active assembling on the 25th ultimo. Assembling of the lining was begun on the 25th ultimo. This will be completed before the vestibule and be shipped at once, to keep the field crew at work, erecting. The workman in charge of the vestibule told me that with all the help he can advantageously employ on it the construction of this vestibule will occupy three months. This length of time, if it can be adhered to, with the necessary time for transportation and erection, would indicate the final completion of the Storage vault as about August first, next.

Details of the progress, as to material and workmanship, were examined in each department of the shops. None of the material put in service since last reports was defective in any manner, and the workmanship was uniformly of the highest class. This applies to the several systems in themselves, only, for no two systems has yet been assembled into their proper places in the whole.

Respectfully,

John P Bergin

Vault, Safe and Lock Expert.

J.P.Bergin,

to the
Supervising Architect.

SUBJECT:

Rel. Inspection of vault work at shops of the Diebold Safe & Lock Co. and estimates of time for delivery in place.

DENVER MINT
M

OFFICE OF SUPERVISING ARCHITECT

IN REPLYING QUOTE UPPER INITIAL RIGHT HAND CORNER

TREASURY DEPARTMENT

WASHINGTON Mar. 2, 1904.

Diebold Safe & Lock Company,

Canton, Ohio.

Gentlemen:

Attention is invited to the contract with you for the supply of certain vaults for the U. S. Mint building at Denver, Colo., which requires completion within 18 months from December 15,1902, the date of approval of your bond.

From a report of an Inspector who has recently visited your shops, it appears that the construction of these vaults is in a backward condition and that there is probability of your failure to complete withinthe time specified.

The office wishes to impress upon you that there is urgent necessity for the completion of all this vault work within the time provided for in your contract, and that it will be to your interest to employ the largest force possible and have these vaults installed complete by June 15th, next, especially in view of the provision of your contract for liquidated damages for each and every day's delay beyond the time provided for.

It is requested that you will make reply to this letter and state what action you have taken to insure the fulfillment of your agreement in all respects.

Respectfully,

(Signed) J. K. Taylor

Supervising Architect.

DENVER, NEW MINT.

OFFICE OF SUPERVISING ARCHITECT

IN REPLYING, QUOTE UPPER INITIAL, RIGHT HAND CORNER

32

TREASURY DEPARTMENT

WASHINGTON March 3, 1904.

Inclosure No. 468.

Superintendent of Construction,
New Mint Building,
Denver, Colorado.

Sir:-

There is inclosed herewith, for your information and the files of your office, copy of Department letter of even date, accepting the proposal of The Diebold Safe & Lock Company to substitute forged steel for pressure bar housings required by their contract for safety vaults and incidental work at the building in your charge, provided no expense is entailed thereby.

Respectfully,

Supervising Architect.

KCH

DENVER, NEW MINT.

March 5, 1904.

Diebold Safe & Lock Company,

Canton, Ohio.

Gentlemen:-

Referring further to your letter of the 24th ultimo, and to your request to substitute forged steel for pressure bar housings required by your contract for safety vaults and incidental work at the new Mint building at Denver, Colorado, you are advised that you will be permitted to make such change provided no expense is entailed thereby, a public exigency requiring them.

It is understood and agreed that this acceptance is not to affect the time for the completion of the entire work as required by the terms of your contract; that the same is without prejudice to any and all rights of the United States thereunder; and without prejudice, also, to any and all rights of the United States against the sureties on the bond executed for the faithful fulfillment of the contract.

Please promptly acknowledge receipt of this letter, a copy of which has been forwarded to the Superintendent.

Respectfully,

Assistant Secretary.

DENVER, NEW MINT.

OFFICE OF SUPERVISING ARCHITECT

IN REPLYING QUOTE UPPER INITIAL, RIGHT HAND CORNER

33

TREASURY DEPARTMENT

WASHINGTON March 4, 1904.

Superintendent of Construction,
New Mint Building,
Denver, Colo.

Sir:-

I have to acknowledge receipt of your letter of the 26th ultimo, relative to certain trim on corridor side of elevator door frames in basement of the building in your charge, and you are advised that wooden trim to correspond with the other trim in corridor is required. While cast iron would have been better, it is believed that, as the contract drawings indicate wood for trim and cast iron jambs, the cast iron can not be demanded for trim.

Respectfully,

Supervising Architect.

KCH

DENVER, NEW MINT.

OFFICE OF SUPERVISING ARCHITECT

IN REPLYING QUOTE UPPER INITIAL. RIGHT HAND CORNER

324

TREASURY DEPARTMENT

WASHINGTON March 5,1904.

Enclosure 1970.

Superintendent of Construction,
New Mint,
Denver, Colorado.

Sir:

Enclosed for your information find copy of a report dated the 23rd ultimo, in relation to the condition of work under the contract with S.Faith and Company, for the mechanical equipment for the building under your charge. There is also enclosed copy of a letter this day addressed to the contractors, in regard to their work, which will explain itself.

You are requested to keep the record, therein indicated, as to the number of days delay for which the contractors are responsible, in order that this feature may be of record when the office is presenting the case to the Hon.Secretary of the Treasury at time of final settlement.

You are also requested, on the 20th instant, to submit a report indicating whether the contractors have given effect to the demand.

Respectfully,

Supervising Architect.

OFFICE OF

SUPERINTENDENT OF Construction,

U. S. Mint Building,

Denver, Colo., February 23rd,1904.

Mr.J.K.Taylor,

Supervising Architect,

Treasury Department, Washington, D.C.

Sir:-

In compliance with instructions in Department letter (initial F. B.W.) of the 5th instant, I have the honor to submit this my weekly report.

S.Faith & Company,Philadelphia,Pennsylvania,contractors for the Mechanical Equipment of the Mint Building,in this city.

Work installed: Plumbing all roughed in,except terra cotta stacks.

Heating mains and returns completed. Heating plant generally,about 30% completed.

Radiators all connected,except in basement.

Boiler feed pumps set,

Vacuum pumps set.

Feed water heater set.

Blow off tank set.

Drip tank set.

Economizer completed,except pipe connections.

Draft fan and stack set up.

Coiner's waste water well completed.

Melter's " " " "

Artesian well drilled to depth of 375 feet, and 6 1/4" casing installed to depth of 320 feet.

Elevator machines in place and a portion of overhead work. Elevator work generally, about 30% completed.

Marble work in toilet rooms, 30% completed.

Ash hoist, completed.

Electric work, 85% completed.

The flooring for toilet rooms in basement and attic could have been put in place more than a month ago, but no work has yet been done in this connection.

I most respectfully call the attention of the Office to the slow progress being made by S. Faith & Company, contractors, and believe that unless material is received more promptly and work executed with more diligence, they will not complete their contract before October, next, notwithstanding the fact that their contract time expired nearly a year ago. A portion of the boilers has been received, but no one is here either to contract for or lay the foundation for the boiler settings, and I most respectfully recommend that S. Faith & Company, contractors, be notified to complete their contract without further delay.

Respectfully,

W. O. Saville.

Inspector, Heating, Hoisting and Ventilating Apparatus.

Forwarded through the

Superintendent of Construction.

Lee Ulery.

Office of Superintendent of Construction

U.S. Mint Building

Denver, Colo

Feb 23, 1904

W. O. Saville

~~Superintendent.~~ Inspector, H H & V. Apparatus

SUBJECT:

Report progress of work on Mechanical Equipment.

TREASURY DEPARTMENT,
RECEIVED.
... 26 ...
Office of Supervising Architect.

Duplicate

No. of Inclosures, ... 26 1904

DENVER, NEW MINT.

OFFICE OF SUPERVISING ARCHITECT

IN REPLYING QUOTE UPPER INITIAL, RIGHT HAND CORNER

TREASURY DEPARTMENT

WASHINGTON March 5, 1904.

Messrs. S. Faith and Company,
2427 Pennsylvania Avenue,
Philadelphia, Pennsylvania.

Sirs:

Referring to your contract for the mechanical equipment, &c., at the U. S. Mint (New), Denver, Colorado, your attention is called to the following extract from a report, submitted to the office, under date of the 23rd ultimo, by the Inspector of Heating, Hoisting and Ventilating Apparatus, now on detail at the building:

"The flooring for toilet rooms in basement and attic could have been put in place more than a month ago, but no work has yet been done in this connection.

I most respectfully call the attention of the Office to the slow progress being made by S. Faith and Company, contractors, and believe that unless material is received more promptly and work executed with more diligence, they will not complete their contract before October next, notwithstanding the fact that their contract time expired nearly a year ago. A portion of the boilers has been received, but no one is here either to contract for or lay the foundation for the boiler settings, and I most respectfully recommend that S. Faith and Company, contractors, be notified to complete their contract without further delay".

From the above statements, it is obvious that you have not in the past, nor are you at the present time conducting the work in a satisfactory manner, and it would seem that immediate action on your part to arrange for the prompt supply of material and for expedition in the work, to secure its completion at the earliest possible date, is absolutely necessary.

The above quoted statements would seem to refute certain claims made by you of delay caused by the contractors for other branches of the work, and would also seem to emphasize the fact that there was no just cause for the complaint recently made by you that the Superintendent was not treating you fairly in his estimates of payments on account of the work.

A copy of this letter has been transmitted to the Superintendent, in order that he may be in possession of full information when it becomes necessary for him to report, at the time when final adjustment of your account is under consideration, and it would seem, therefore, that to minimize any damages which might accrue for your failure to complete on time, better improvement should be noted in the work from now on than has prevailed since you entered into the agreement.

Respectfully,

(Signed) J.K. Taylor
Supervising Architect.

OWK

DENVER MINT (NEW).

IN REPLYING QUOTE UPPER INITIAL RIGHT HAND CORNER

35

TREASURY DEPARTMENT

WASHINGTON March 5,1904.

Superintendent of Construction,
New Mint Building,
Denver,Colorado.

Sir:

For your information I have to advise you that the Department has this day rejected all the proposals received under advertisement dated January 7,1904 for lighting fixtures for the building in your charge, and new proposals will be invited, based upon revised drawings and specification. You will be duly informed of any action taken.

Respectfully,

Supervising Architect.

JSS

DENVER, NEW MINT

INCLOSURE #3561

376

TREASURY DEPARTMENT

WASHINGTON March 5, 1904.

Superintendent of Construction,
New Mint Building,
Denver, Colorado.

Sir:

There is inclosed herewith, for your information and the files of your office, a copy of Department letter of even date accepting the proposal of Mr. James A. McGonigle, in amount $30.00, for certain terra cotta partition in the attic of the building under your charge, all as set forth in said letter of acceptance.

You are hereby authorized to certify and issue vouchers on account of the work in accordance with the terms of the contract and the printed "Instructions to Superintendents," payment of which vouchers the Disbursing Agent has this day been authorized to make from the appropriation for Mint Building, Denver, Colorado.

Respectfully,

J K Taylor
Supervising Architect.

HM

DENVER, NEW MINT

March 5, 1904.

Mr. James A. McGonigle,
New Mint Building,
Denver, Colorado.

Sir:

In view of the statement and recommendation contained in letter dated February 26, 1904, from the Superintendent of Construction of the new Mint building at Denver, Colorado, your proposal, addressed to him, in amount thirty dollars ($30.00), is hereby accepted for certain terra cotta partition in the attic of said building, the amount being deemed reasonable and a public exigency requiring this addition to your contract for the construction of the building.

It is understood and agreed that this acceptance is not to affect the time for the completion of the work as required by the terms of your contract, that the same is without prejudice to any and all rights of the United States thereunder; and without prejudice, also, to any and all rights of the United States against the sureties on the bond executed for the faithful fulfillment of the contract.

Please promptly acknowledge receipt of this letter, a copy of which will be sent to the Superintendent for his information.

Respectfully,

Assistant Secretary.

T.
J.B.P.

MB

[illegible]

[illegible]

[illegible]

[illegible]

[illegible]

[illegible]

[illegible]

[illegible]

DENVER, NEW MINT.

OFFICE OF SUPERVISING ARCHITECT

IN REPLYING QUOTE UPPER INITIAL, RIGHT HAND CORNER.

39

TREASURY DEPARTMENT

WASHINGTON March 5, 1904.

Inclosure No. 476.

Superintendent of Construction,
New Mint Building,
Denver, Colorado.

Sir:-

There is inclosed herewith, for your information and the files of your office, copy of Department letter of even date, accepting the proposal of James A. McGonigle, to deduct ten dollars ($10.00), from his contract for the completion of the building, for omitting certain T irons required at the meeting rails of fourteen basement windows in the building in your charge.

Respectfully,

J. K. Taylor
Supervising Architect.

KCH

DENVER, NEW MINT.

March 8, 1904.

James A. McGonigle,
New Mint Building,
Denver, Colorado.

Sir:-

In view of the statements and recommendation contained in letter of the 25th ultimo, from the Superintendent of Construction for the New Mint Building, Denver, Colorado, your proposal of February 24, 1904, to deduct ten dollars ($10.00), from your contract for the completion of the building, on account of omitting certain T irons required on the meeting rails of fourteen basement windows, is hereby accepted, the amount being deemed reasonable and a public exigency requiring the change in the work.

It is understood and agreed that this acceptance is not to affect the time for the completion of the entire work as required by the terms of your contract; that the same is without prejudice to any and all rights of the United States thereunder; and without prejudice, also, to any and all rights of the United States against the sureties on the bond executed for the faithful fulfillment of the contract.

Please promptly acknowledge receipt of this letter, a copy of which is forwarded to the Superintendent.

Respectfully,

Assistant Secretary.

T.

(PRINTED HEADING).

Denver, Colo., March 10,1904.

Mr.Lee Ullery,

Supt.Mint Building,

Denver.

Dear Sir:-

Your letter of February 16th asking for bid to enclose the group of electric wire conduits in boiler room received. I will furnish material and labor and do it according to your letter of instruction for $120.00, using Loveland plaster or using asbestos for $150.

Yours truly,

(Signed) James A.McGonigle.

(PRINTED HEADING). 41

Philadelphia, March 8,1904.

Mr.Lee Ullery,

Supt. Construction, U.S.Mint Building,

Denver, Colorado.

Dear Sir:-

Answering yours of 3rd. instant, we propose to furnish all labor and material for live steam piping to gas generating room,in building under your charge, for the sum of TWENTY NINE DOLLARS($29.00).

If live steam piping to Fuel Gas Generating Room is omitted, deduct the sum of ELEVEN DOLLARS from our contract price.

Awaiting your most favorable consideration, we remain

Yours respectfully,

(Signed) S.Faith & Company,

S.

DENVER NEW MINT.

OFFICE OF SUPERVISING ARCHITECT

IN REPLYING QUOTE UPPER INITIAL, RIGHT HAND CORNER

42

TREASURY DEPARTMENT

5

WASHINGTON March 12,1904.

Superintendent of Construction,
U. S. Mint (New),
Denver, Colorado.

Sir:

Referring to the statements contained in your letter of the 29th ultimo, in relation to the method of jointing certain joinery work to be supplied under the contract with Mr. James A. McGonigle, for the interior finish, &c., at the building under your charge, you are advised that the method found to exist at the mills, as recently reported by a representative of the office, is considered objectionable, as the class of work called for by the specification is such that it does not permit of joints showing on backs of trims. There is no objection, however, to jointing the trim, provided joints are concealed.

Respectfully,

Supervising Architect.

Forwarding.

March 12,1904.

Mr. James A. McGonigle,
Leavenworth, Kansas.

Sir:

In view of the statement and recommendation contained in letter of the 20th ultimo, from the Superintendent of Construction of the new Mint Building, Denver, Colorado, and in accordance with the approval of this Department, your proposal, dated the 17th ultimo, addressed to him, in amount seven thousand eight hundred and eighty-five dollars ($7,885.00), is hereby accepted, as an addition to your contract, dated August 25,1902, for the completion of the building, to furnish all the labor and materials required to complete a storage cellar for sweeps at the west end of the building, in accordance with drawing #247-A (copy of which is forwarded herewith), and the terms of the superintendent's letter to you of the 1st ultimo, a public exigency requiring the immediate performance of the work.

It is understood and agreed that this acceptance is not to affect the time for the completion of the work as required by the terms of your contract; that the same is without prejudice to any and all rights of the United States thereunder; and without prejudice, also, to any and all rights of the United States against the sureties on the bond executed for the faithful fulfillment of the contract.

Please acknowledge the receipt of this letter.

Respectfully,

Superintendent of Construction,

U. S. Mint,

Denver, Colo.

Sir:

In connection with office letter addressed to you on the 9th instant in relation to this matter, please find inclosed herewith for your information and the files of your office a copy of a letter of the 10th instant from the Diebold Safe & Lock Co., regarding the reinforcement of floors of vaults to be supplied by them and of reply thereto of even date.

Should there be evidence of any further unbusinesslike methods on the part of this Company in the installation of these vaults, advise this office fully in regard thereto, with such recommendations as you deem proper.

Respectfully,

Supervising Architect.

DENVER MINT

OFFICE OF SUPERVISING ARCHITECT

IN REPLYING, QUOTE UPPER INITIAL, RIGHT HAND CORNER.

TREASURY DEPARTMENT

WASHINGTON March 12, 1904.

The Diebold Safe & Lock Company,

Canton, Ohio.

Gentlemen:

Your communication of the 10th instant has been received in relation to reinforcing floors of certain vaults in the new mint building at Denver, Colo.

In view of the letter which was addressed to you on the 18th ultimo by the Superintendent of Construction, it was assumed that you had full information in regard to the conditions complained of. It is hoped, however, you have taken decided action in the matter, and will have this preliminary work completed without further delay.

A copy of your letter has been forwarded to the Superintendent for his information, with instructions to keep the office advised in the premises.

Respectfully,

(Signed) J. K. Taylor

Supervising Architect.

COPY. Printed heading.

Canton, Ohio, March 10th, 1904.

Jas. Knox Taylor, Esq.,

Supervising Architect,

Treasury Department,

Washington, D. C.

Dear Sir:

We are in receipt of your favor of the 9th inst., signed by the Assistant Secretary, concerning Vault work for the U. S. Mint Building, at Denver, Colo.

We are greatly surprised at the contents of your letter, as we have no information concerning the condition of affairs as stated. Our representative, Mr. Philip Garretson, was given instructions to have the sub-structures for Vaults E.F.G.& M. placed without delay; and he notified us recently that there was likely to be some trouble between the Union and Non-Union labor. We at once advised him to see that the work proceeded without delay, and up to this time have no further advice from him, consequently assumed that the work was being satisfactorily completed.

We are writing Mr. Garretson today, instructing him to have the work pushed to completion as rapidly as possible, and that the necessary competent mechanics be employed to do this work. Please be assured that this work will be pushed to completion without further delay. We very much regret the existing condition, as stated by you the proper remedy will be immediately applied.

Very respectfully,
(Signed) F. C. Baehrens,
Secy.

DENVER NEW MINT.

45

TREASURY DEPARTMENT

5

OFFICE OF SUPERVISING ARCHITECT

IN REPLYING QUOTE UPPER INITIAL RIGHT HAND CORNER

WASHINGTON March 12, 1904.

FBW

Enclosure 690.

Superintendent of Construction,
U. S. Mint (New),
Denver, Colorado.

Sir:

Referring to the statements contained in your letter of the 7th instant, in relation to estimates of payments and the condition of work, under the contract with Messrs. S. Faith and Company, for the mechanical equipment, &c., at the building under your charge, there is transmitted herewith copy of a letter this day addressed to the contractors named, which will explain itself.

It is requested that you keep careful record of all delays in the work, in order that it may be determined at time of final settlement the extent of the delay for which the contractors are responsible.

Respectfully,

Supervising Architect.

DENVER NEW MINT.

OFFICE OF SUPERVISING ARCHITECT

TREASURY DEPARTMENT

S
7/3N

WASHINGTON March 12, 1904.

IN REPLYING QUOTE UPPER INITIAL, RIGHT HAND CORNER

Copy

Enclosure 689.

Messrs. S. Faith and Company,
2427 Pennsylvania Avenue,
Philadelphia, Pennsylvania.

Sirs:

Your letter of the 7th instant, is hereby acknowledged, in which you attempt to explain the causes for the unsatisfactory condition of work under your contract for the mechanical equipment, &c., at the U. S. Mint (New), at Denver, Colorado.

The statements made by you are noted, but reports received from the Superintendent and from the Inspector now on duty at the building, indicate quite clearly that the work is not being prosecuted in a connected and businesslike manner, such as is required by the terms of your contract, and as evidence of this, there is transmitted herewith a letter, dated the 7th instant, received from the Superintendent at the building.

As you are aware, the contract time for the completion of your work, has long since expired, and while it is possible that additional time is due you for certain delays caused by the Government, yet the records disclose the fact that other delays have occurred and are now taking place for which you alone are responsible and which must receive the attention of the Department, under the clause of the contract providing for liquidated damages, at time of final settlement.

As stated in office letter of the 2nd instant, in response to your complaint as the unfairness of the Superintendent in his estimates of payments on account of the work, to the effect that you claim compensation for work and material set in place complete, it is proper to note that the Superintendent, in his letter, bears out this fact, and from the tenor of his report, it would seem that the Government has promptly met its obligations to you as set forth in the contract.

A copy of this letter has been forwarded to the Superintendent at the building, for his information and guidance, with directions to keep a careful record of all delays, and especially those for which you are responsible, in order that the same may be of record when final settlement is being considered.

It is proper to state, in this connection, that the office is prepared at all times to carefully consider any complaints or statements made by you, which may have bearing in fact, but it quite agrees with the Superintendent in the position taken by him that your interests would be better subserved by the prompt and satisfactory installation of your work, rather than by correspondence setting forth conditions that do not actually exist.

Respectfully,

James K. Taylor

Supervising Architect.

Cdl L

Treasury Department.

[illegible]

Washington, D.C., March 10, 1904.

Superintendent of Construction,
Mint Building,
Denver, Colo.

Sir:

[illegible] required [illegible] of

March [illegible], [illegible] the work [illegible] has been

received and you are advised that a remittance of $ 45,000.00

to the Disbursing Agent has been requested.

Respectfully,

[illegible]

[illegible]

FAP

TREASURY DEPARTMENT

March 9,

Superintendent of Construction,
New Mint Building,
Denver, Colorado.

Sir:

I have to acknowledge receipt of your letter of the 7th instant, inclosing proposal from F. Wagner's Company, in a seven hundred and twenty-five dollars ($725.00), for substituting flush type instruments in lieu of those required by contract, in connection with the switchboard in the Buildi in your charge, and you are directed to reject their prop as it is considered excessive and to instruct the contrac to install switches as required by their contract for the mechanical equipment of the building.

You are also directed to call the attention of the contractors to paragraph 804 of the specification, requiring switchboard to be inspected in the shop when set up [illegible] and to inform them that any instruments now in Denver to mounted on said board must be shipped to Reading where th is being built for mounting.

Respectfully,

DENVER MINT

OFFICE OF SUPERVISING ARCHITECT

IN REPLYING QUOTE UPPER INITIAL RIGHT HAND CORNER

Inclosure 1310.

TREASURY DEPARTMENT

48

S

WASHINGTON March 9, 1904. Jaw

Superintendent of Construction,

U. S. Mint,

Denver, Colo.

Sir:

Referring to your communication of the 5th instant and telegram of the 8th instant in relation to vault work in the building under your charge, please find inclosed herewith a copy of Department letter of this date addressed to the Diebold Safe & Lock Co., which explains itself.

It is requested that you will keep the office advised of the action of the contractors in complying with this demand, and on the 19th instant submit a report as to whether the work has been completed, together with any recommendations which you may deem proper in the premises.

In connection with the concluding paragraph of your letter you are informed that it is the declared policy of the Department not to interfere in the matter of labor unions, requiring only that the contractors perform their work as provided for in their contracts.

Respectfully,

L — J. K. Taylor

Supervising Architect.

DENVER MINT
M

In replying to this letter the initials in upper right-hand corner must be referred to.

TREASURY DEPARTMENT,

OFFICE OF THE SECRETARY,

Washington, March 9, 1904.

The Diebold Safe & Lock Company,

Canton, Ohio.

Gentlemen:

Referring to your contract for the installation of vaults in the U. S. Mint at Denver, Colo., your attention now is particularly invited to that portion providing for the reinforcement of the floors of vaults E, F, G and M, which work must be so conducted by you that the walls around the vaults may be built whenever required by the Superintendent.

A report has just been received from the Superintendent to the effect that he has been unsuccessful in his endeavors to secure from you the completion of this work, in order that the terra cotta walls inclosing the vaults may be constructed and certain other contingent work included in another contract completed; that you have had a few boys employed, whose employment has resulted in a strike on the part of the other mechanics in the building and generally disorganized and interfered with the progress of work.

The Department must express surprise that you have permitted such a condition of affairs in a matter of this kind, especially in view of the clause on page 5 of the specification requiring that "the work must be executed in such a manner as in the judgment of the Superintendent of the building will interfere the least with the operations of other contractors in the building and yet proceed with all reasonable speed," and your action does not in any manner reflect credit upon you.

It has been decided not to tolerate any longer this unbusiness-like manner of conducting the work, and demand is now made upon you to complete the reinforcement of the floors of vaults F, G and M and repair the terra cotta and other work damaged by you by the 19th instant.

This demand is made under rights reserved to the Government in paragraph included in lines 42 to 56 on page 3 of the contract, and in the event of your failure to complete the work as called for within the time allowed, further action will be taken under the rights reserved in that paragraph, with a view to protecting the Government's interests.

A copy of this letter will be sent to the Superintendent of Construction at the building with instructions to keep the Department advised in the premises.

Respectfully,

(Signed) C. H. Keep.

S
T

Assistant Secretary.

DENVER MINT, NEW.

49

OFFICE OF SUPERVISING ARCHITECT

TREASURY DEPARTMENT FBW

WASHINGTON March 15, 1904.

IN REPLYING, QUOTE UPPER INITIAL, RIGHT HAND CORNER

(ENCLOSURE #62)

The Superintendent of Construction,

U.S. Mint Building,

Denver, Colorado.

Sir:

There is enclosed herewith a copy of Office letter this day addressed to Mr. James A. McGonigle, relative to the border for first story corridor floor in the building for which you are the Superintendent of Construction, which will explain itself.

Respectfully,

J K Taylor
Supervising Architect.

B.

DENVER MINT, NEW.

IN REPLYING TO THIS LETTER THE INITIALS IN UPPER RIGHT-HAND CORNER MUST BE REFERRED TO.

TREASURY DEPARTMENT,

OFFICE OF THE SUPERVISING ARCHITECT,

Washington, March 15, 1904.

Mr. James A. McGonigle,

U.S. Mint Building,

Denver, Colorado.

Sir:

The receipt of your telegram of March 14th, relative to of first story corridor floor, new U.S. Mint Building, Denver, Colorado, is hereby acknowledged, and in reply you were this day wired as follows:

> "Drawing border first story corridor floor will be forwarded. Different from entrance hall. No sample necessary. Letter."

A drawing is now being prepared and will be forwarded at once, showing the design desired for the borders of the corridor, first floor, which will be different in design from the border used in the entrance hall.

It will be unnecessary to submit a sample, as in color and execution this work is to agree with the sample already approved for entrance hall.

Respectfully,

J. K. TAYLOR

Supervising Architect.

B.

TELEPHONE CONNECTION.

THE UNITED STATES MINT, PHILADELPHIA. HEATING, VENTILATING & PLUMBING INSTALLED BY S. FAITH & CO.

S. Faith & Co.

Contractors

FOR

Steam & Hot Water Heating

Plumbing & Ventilating Apparatus

OFFICE 2427-33 PENNSYLVANIA AVENUE

THE WITHERSPOON BUILDING, PHILADELPHIA. PLUMBING INSTALLED BY S. FAITH & CO.

COUNTRY WORK PROMPTLY ATTENDED TO

Philadelphia March 18th. 1904 190

Mr. Lee Ullery,

Supt. of Construction,

U. S. Mint, Denver, Colo.

Dear sir:--

Relative to the marble work for the building under your charge, in toilet room #2 the plans show a distance of 4'-0" from shower partition to wall, and we roughed in accordingly. The marble plans show this space to be 5'-0". This is a mistake of the Government and we will be compelled to install same correctly and therefore must look for an extra for same.

In toilet room #3 the plans show 3'-0" for closet enclousure and marble plan shows 2'-6" causing another change in our work. This also will be an extra.

In the meantime we will instruct our man to go ahead with work.

Yours respectfully,

C.F.S./.H

DENVER MINT, NEW.

4 50
Fow

OFFICE OF SUPERVISING ARCHITECT

IN REPLYING, QUOTE UPPER INITIAL, RIGHT HAND CORNER.

TREASURY DEPARTMENT

WASHINGTON March 17, 1904.

FORWARDING.
ENCLOSURE-77.

The Superintendent of Construction,

New Mint Building,

Denver, Colorado.

Sir:

There is enclosed herewith for your information and files, a copy of office letter this day addressed to Mr. James A. McGonigle, and, under separate cover, a copy of full size detail drawing No.269, therein mentioned, in connection with the mosaic borders to be installed in the first story corridor of the building for which you are the Superintendent of Construction, and you will please be governed accordingly.

Respectfully,

M.

Supervising Architect.

DENVER MINT, N.W.

TREASURY DEPARTMENT,

OFFICE OF THE SUPERVISING ARCHITECT.

In replying to this letter the initials in upper right hand corner must be referred to

Washington, March 17, 1904.

FORWARDING.
ENCLOSURE-78.

Mr. James A. McGonigle,

Leavenworth,

Kansas.

Sir:

In accordance with the request contained in your telegram of the 15th instant, there has been prepared and this day forwarded to the above address a copy of drawing No.269; being the full size detail for the mosaic border to be installed under the contract for the interior finish in the first story corridor of the New U.S.Mint Building, Denver, Colorado.

An additional copy of the above mentioned drawing has also been forwarded, in accordance with your request, to the New England Mosaic Company, 36 Chardon Street, Boston, Massachusetts.

Respectfully,

J. K. TAYLOR,

Supervising Architect.

M.

DENVER, NEW MINT.

OFFICE OF SUPERVISING ARCHITECT

IN REPLYING QUOTE UPPER INITIAL RIGHT HAND CORNER

INCLOSURE #1066

TREASURY DEPARTMENT

51

WASHINGTON March 17, 1904.

Superintendent of Construction,
New Mint Building,
Denver, Colorado.

Sir:

There is inclosed herewith, for your information, a copy of a letter of even date relative to cesspool in connection with the building under your charge, which is self-explanatory.

Respectfully,

J. K. Taylor
Supervising Architect.

DENVER, NEW MINT

March 17, 1904.

Messrs. S. Faith & Company,
#8427 Pennsylvania Avenue,
Philadelphia, Pennsylvania.

Gentlemen:

Your proposal of the 12th instant to deduct the sum of $2.00 from the amount to be paid you under your contract for mechanical equipment at the new Mint building, Denver, Colorado, for making certain change in cesspool referred to in paragraph 152 of the specification, is rejected, and you are advised that a special cast iron cesspool with 8" outlet or a heavy cast iron frame and grating, similar to Mott's plate 292-S (stable catalogue), set on a brick catch basin having an 8" outlet connection, with quarter bend turned down inside to form trap, will be acceptable.

You are further advised that all proposals of this description should be forwarded through the office of the Superintendent of Construction and not direct to this office.

Respectfully,

Supervising Architect.

HM

J 2

James A.McGonigle,

Contractor and Builder,

Leavenworth, Kansas,March 19,1904.

Mr.Lee Ullery,
Supt. New Mint, Denver, Colorado.

Dear Sir:-

Referring to your letter of the 15th instant,in regards to jointing the inside trim at doors and windows and the ruling of the Supervising Architect.

Will you please ask Supervising Architect for a rehearing and reversal of his ruling in regard to jointing trim in view of the following:

1. April 29th,1903. The department wrote under initials "T.B.W." in answer to my verbal request of April 27th,paragraph 6 and 7. "In many cases the wood finish is shown as a whole not detailed in pieces, the question of jointing being left to the judgment of the contractor".

2. The entire finish is now made filled and varnished ready to load in car at St.Louis,having been made in accordance with the best judgment of this contractor(for use in a building of this character in many cases occurring in rooms subject to severe usage) in two pieces carefully jointed thus:

In many cases the outer edge butts against plaster jamb entirely concealing joints. In other cases where there is no plaster jamb the rooms are small and fifficult to obtain view of outer edge. In no case does trim occur in corridor of principal stories.

3. The the building is now ready to receive trim and it will cause serious delay to make the change it is respectfully requested that the Department allow this trim to be used. The material has been inspected by Mr.G.B.Strickler the Department representative at the Louisiana Purchase Exposition in St.Louis, and we think he will report that it has been manufactured in the best manner of a superior quality of quartered white oak and unusual precaution taken to kiln dry and insure its reaching the building with less moisture than test specified

4. As the building is now ready to receive this trim an immediate consideration of this matter will greatly oblige,

Yours respectfully,

(Signed) James A.McGonigle.

DENVER, NEW MINT.

S 3

OFFICE OF SUPERVISING ARCHITECT

IN REPLYING, QUOTE UPPER INITIAL, RIGHT HAND CORNER.

TREASURY DEPARTMENT

WASHINGTON

March 19, 1904.

Superintendent of Construction,

Mint Building,

Denver, Colo.

Sir:

Replying to your letter of the 14th instant, relative to advances made to the Disbursing Agent, etc., I have to advise you that a warrant in amount $45,000.00 was issued today and will be mailed at once to the Disbursing Agent.

In this connection I have to advise you that no amount in excess of the Disbursing Agent's bond can be sent him, but it is suggested, if the conditions warrant, that the Disbursing Agent submit a supplemental account to this office about the middle of the month, which should include all expenditures made to that date, and upon the receipt of same immediate action will be taken to put further funds in his hands.

Respectfully,

Chief Executive Officer.

FAB

DENVER, NEW MINT

OFFICE OF SUPERVISING ARCHITECT

IN REPLYING, QUOTE UPPER INITIAL, RIGHT HAND CORNER.

INCLOSURE #1075

TREASURY DEPARTMENT

WASHINGTON March 19, 1904.

Superintendent of Construction,
New Mint Building,
Denver, Colorado.

Sir:

There is inclosed herewith, for your information and the files of your office, a copy of Department letter of even date accepting the proposal of Messrs. S. Faith & Company, same being an addition of $29.00 to their contract for the mechanical equipment for the building under your charge, and a deduction of $11.00 from said contract, on account of certain steam piping, all as set forth in said letter of acceptanc You are hereby authorized to certify and issue vouchers on account of the above, stating the two items separately, in accordance with the terms of the contract and the printed "Instructions to Superintendents," payment of which vouchers the Disbursing Agent has this day been authorized to make from the appropriation for Mint Building, Denver, Colorado.

Respectfully,

Supervising Architect.

HM

March 19,1904.

Messrs. S. Faith & Company,
#2427 Pennsylvania Avenue,
Philadelphia, Pennsylvania.

Gentlemen:

In view of the statement and recommendation contained in letter dated March 11,1904, from the Superintendent of Construction of the new Mint building at Denver, Colorado, your proposal, dated March 8,1904, addressed to him, is hereby accepted as follows:

For furnishing all the labor and material required to run live steam piping to gas generating room in said building......................1......$29.00
For omitting to run live steam piping to fuel gas generator room.................. DEDUCT 11.00
Net amount......$18.00

The amount is deemed reasonable and a public exigency requires the immediate performance of the work which is considered as an addition to your contract for mechanical equipment at the said building.

It is understood and agreed that this acceptance is not to affect the time for the completion of the work as required by the terms of your contract; that the same is without prejudice to any and all rights of the United States thereunder; and without prejudice, also, to any and all rights of the United States against the sureties on the bond executed for the faithful fulfillment of the contract.

Respectfully,

~~Assistant~~ Actg. Secretary.

T.
J.C.P.
HM

DENVER, MINT (new)

OFFICE OF SUPERVISING ARCHITECT

IN REPLYING QUOTE UPPER INITIAL, RIGHT HAND CORNER

S S

TREASURY DEPARTMENT FBW

WASHINGTON March 21, 1904.

The Superintendent of Construction,

New Mint Building,

Denver, Colorado.

Sir:

The receipt of your letter of the 12th instant relative to the masterkeying of the locks for the doors of the building for which you are the Superintendent of Construction, is hereby acknowledged.

In reply you are informed that the Assayer-in-charge of the United States Mint at Denver, will undoubtedly be appointed Custodian of the new Mint, and you are directed to take the matter up with him and settle it immediately.

Respectfully,

J. K. Taylor

Supervising Architect.

R.

DENVER NEW MINT.

Inclosure 955.

TREASURY DEPARTMENT

56

WASHINGTON March 25, 1904.

IN REPLYING, QUOTE UPPER INITIAL RIGHT HAND CORNER

Superintendent of Construction,
New Mint Building,
Denver, Colo.

Sir:

I inclose herewith, for your information and the files of your office, a copy of Department letter of even date, accepting the proposal of James A. McGonigle, in amount one hundred and fifty dollars ($150.00), as an addition to his contract for the completion of the building in your charge, to cover with asbestos the feeder conduits at ceiling of boiler room; and you are hereby authorized to certify and issue vouchers for the work, as required by the terms of the contract and the printed "Instructions to Superintendents", payment of which vouchers the Disbursing Agent has been authorized to make from the appropriation for Mint Building, Denver, Colorado.

FAB

Respectfully,

Supervising Architect.

JSS

DENVER, NEW MINT.

March 23, 1904.

Mr. James A. McGonigle,
U.S. Mint Building,
Denver, Colorado.

Sir:

In view of the statement and recommendation contained in letter of the 11th instant, from the Superintendent of Construction of the new Mint Building at Denver, Colorado, and in accordance with the approval of this Department, your proposal, of the 10th instant, addressed to him, in amount one hundred and fifty dollars ($150.00), is hereby accepted, as an addition to your contract dated August 25, 1902 for the completion of the building, to cover with asbestos feeder conduits at ceiling of boiler room, in accordance with the terms of the superintendent's letter to you of the 10th ultimo, and to his satisfaction, a public exigency requiring the immediate performance of the work.

It is understood and agreed that this acceptance is not to affect the time for the completion of the work as required by the terms of your contract; that the same is without prejudice to any and all rights of the United States thereunder, and without prejudice, also, to any and all rights of the United States against the sureties on the bond executed for the faithful fulfillment of the contract.

Please acknowledge the receipt of this letter.

Respectfully,

Acting Secretary.

[illegible]

[illegible] Mar[illegible]

[illegible]

[illegible]

To [illegible]

[illegible] (N-W),

[illegible]

[illegible]

[illegible] will be [illegible]

[illegible]

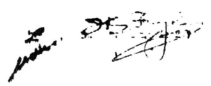

DENVER (NEW) MINT.

MEMO

March 22, 1904.

FORWARDING.

Messrs. S. Smith and Company,

2467 Pennsylvania Avenue,

Philadelphia, Pa.

Sirs:

Referring to your contract for mechanical equipment of the U. S. Mint (new), Denver, Col., receipt is acknowledged of your letter of the 21st instant, enclosing print (in triplicate) showing said fume fan, submitted in lieu of drawing of same fan approved August 15, 1903, and given office number M-221.

The drawing is approved as now submitted, and has been given office number M-221 A. Copy is forwarded to you herewith, under separate cover.

Respectfully,

(Signed) [illegible]

Supervising Architect.

(DENVER (new) MINT)

S 9

OFFICE OF SUPERVISING ARCHITECT

IN REPLYING, QUOTE UPPER INITIAL, RIGHT HAND CORNER

TREASURY DEPARTMENT FBW

WASHINGTON March 24, 1904.

The Superintendent of Construction,

United States (new) Mint Building,

Denver, Colorado.

Sir:

The office is in receipt of two photographs representing the models for plaster work to be used in connection with the interior finish of the building for which you are the Superintendent of Construction.

In this connection you are advised that while the sheet marked No.1 is satisfactory, that marked #2, which shows the large cartouche for corners of cornice, is not, and must be made to correspond in every way with the model furnished for this work by the Government.

These photographs are, apparently, taken from plaster casts, and you should direct the contractors attention to the fact the specification clearly states that the photographs are to be taken from the models before casting, in other words, from the clay.

Respectfully,

J K Taylor
Supervising Architect.

R.

[illegible] Superintendent of Construction,
[illegible] New Mint,
Denver, Colorado.

Sir:

Referring to the statements contained in your letter of [illegible] instant, and its enclosures, in relation to the joint[illegible] of [illegible] metal trim, as arranged in the contract with Mr. [illegible] [illegible], for the interior finish of the building under your charge, your attention is called to the following paragraph [illegible] letter addressed to the contractor on April [illegible], 190[illegible], copy of which was transmitted to you on the same day.

"I said, [illegible] in many cases the trim finish is shown as a [illegible] - not detailed in pieces - the question of jointing [illegible] left [illegible] the judgment of the contractor".

As it would appear, therefore, that the full size details did not disclose the method of jointing this trim, and as the matter was left [illegible] the judgment of the contractor, no objection will be interposed by the office [illegible] its installation as now prepared, provided that in all other respects the quality of [illegible] material and character of workmanship fulfill the requirements of the agreement.

It is understood by the office that the amount of jointing in question is small, and the office looks to you to see that [illegible] work when installed is satisfactory in all respects.

Please advise the contractor of the tenor of this letter.

Respectfully,

J K Taylor
Supervising Architect.

JAS

DENVER MINT.

OFFICE OF SUPERVISING ARCHITECT

IN REPLYING, QUOTE UPPER INITIAL, RIGHT HAND CORNER

TREASURY DEPARTMENT

WASHINGTON March 28, 1904.

Superintendent of Construction,
New Mint Building,
Denver, Colo.

Sir:-

I have to acknowledge receipt of your letter of the 9th instant, relative to painting copper work in connection with the building in your charge, and you are advised that the contract of James A. McGonigle undoubtedly requires that all exterior copper, under whatever contract placed, is to be painted, and you are directed to obtain a proposal for substituting an acid proof paint for that required by the specification and forward it to this Office with your definite recommendation, together with a sample of the paint, in amount two quarts, for laboratory test.

Respectfully,

J. K. Taylor
Supervising Architect.

KCH

The Mint of the United States at Denver,

Office of the Assayer in charge,

March 29, 1904.

Sir:-

I have to advise you that I am in receipt of a letter from the Secretary of the Treasury informing me of my appointment as Custodian of the Mint Building at Denver, Colorado.

Respectfully yours,

Frank M. Downer

Assayer in Charge.

Mr. Lee Ullery,

Supt. Construction Mint Building,

Denver, Colo.

DENVER (NEW) MINT.

MGD

IN REPLYING, QUOTE UPPER INITIAL, RIGHT HAND CORNER.

J

60

TREASURY DEPARTMENT

WASHINGTON March 29, 1904.

The Superintendent of Construction,

U. S. Mint (New),

Denver, Col.

Sir:

Referring to your letter of the 25th instant, relative to the kind of hose required under paragraph 137 of specification governing the work of mechanical equipment of the building for which you are Superintendent, you are advised that the contractor has submitted samples of fire hose, and action will be taken on same within a few days. You will be duly advised thereof, and furnished with samples.

Respectfully,

Acting Supervising Architect.

DENVER (NEW MINT).

NGD

OFFICE OF SUPERVISING ARCHITECT

IN REPLYING, QUOTE UPPER INITIAL, RIGHT HAND CORNER.

64

TREASURY DEPARTMENT

WASHINGTON March 30, 1904.

ENCLOSURE 4015.

The Superintendent of Construction,

U. S. Mint (New), Denver, Col.

Sir:

For your information find herewith copy of office letter of this date, addressed to S. Faith and Company, contractors for mechanical equipment of the building for which you are Superintendent, approving dove Vermont marble for switchboard, and advising them that the sample switch, approved September 24, 1903, and sent to you, may now be shipped to Reading, Pa., as they request, to be mounted on switchboard.

You are therefore requested to turn said sample switch over to the contractors' representative at the building, first placing thereon a private mark, and notifying this office of same.

Respectfully,

Supervising Architect.

March 30, 1904.

Messrs. S. Faith and Company,

2427 Pennsylvania Avenue,

P Philadelphia, Pa.

Sirs:

Referring to your contract for mechanical equipment of the U. S. Mint (new), Denver, Col., receipt is acknowledged of your letter of the 26th instant, relative to sample switch and marble for switchboard.

In reply you are advised that the sample switch, approved in office letter of September 24, 1903, and forwarded to the Superintendent of Construction at the building, for his guidance, may now be shipped to Reading, Pa., as requested by you, to be mounted on the switchboard. The Superintendent will be instructed to turn the switch over to your representative at the building.

With reference to marble for switchboard, you are advised that the 2' x 4' x 2" sample of dove Vermont marble submitted is approved for use, in lieu of "sample #2" approved in office letter of January 29th last. The new sample will be retained for the information of the Inspector

Respectfully,

(Signed) J.K.Taylor

Supervising Architect.

Treasury Department,

OFFICE OF THE SUPERVISING ARCHITECT.

Washington, D. C., March 30, 1904.

The Superintendent of Construction,

Mint Building, (new),

Denver, Colorado.

Sir:

In view of the request and recommendation contained in your letter of the 25th instant, and the public exigency requiring the immediate delivery of the articles and performance of the work you are hereby authorized to incur an expenditure of thirty-nine dollars and five cents ($39.05)

in securing in open market at lowest prevailing rates

water rent for office for six months from November 1st, 1903,	$ 6.75
ten (10) gallons of coal oil for light,	2.30
telephone service for use of Superintendent for three months from the 1st proximo, at $10.00 per month,	30.00

Your attention is called to printed "Instructions to Superintendents," and you will issue and certify vouchers on account of the above in accordance therewith, payment to be made from the appropriation for "Mint Building, Denver, Colo."

Respectfully.

Chief Executive Officer.

DENVER MINT

M

OFFICE OF SUPERVISING ARCHITECT

IN REPLYING, QUOTE UPPER INITIAL, RIGHT HAND CORNER

Inclosure 1365.

66

TREASURY DEPARTMENT

S

WASHINGTON March 31, 1904.

Superintendent of Construction,

U. S. Mint,

Denver, Colo.

Sir:

There is inclosed herewith for your information and the files of your office a copy of a letter this day addressed to the Diebold Safe & Lock Co., in relation to their contract for the installation of vaults in the building under your charge.

Respectfully,

J. K. Taylor

Supervising Architect.

DENVER MINT
K

OFFICE OF SUPERVISING ARCHITECT

IN REPLYING, QUOTE UPPER INITIAL RIGHT HAND CORNER

TREASURY DEPARTMENT

WASHINGTON March 31, 1904

The Diebold Safe & Lock Co.,

Canton, Ohio.

Gentlemen:

Your communication of the 28th instant is received in which you state with reference to your contract for the installation of vaults, etc., in the Mint at Denver, Colo., that you "expect to make shipment of vaults E, F, and G in four to five weeks. Vault K will follow in two or three weeks after E, F, and G are shipped."

When the letter was addressed to you on the 25th instant, it was expected you would make a full report in regard to all the work in the contract not yet shipped, and the office regrets that it is necessary to repeat that request, which information it is hoped you will furnish without further delay.

From present indications, it is apparent that you will be considerably behind your contract time in the completion of this work, and a due regard for your interests would seem to prompt you in handling this matter in a more business like manner than appears to be the case from the records here. As an instance, there may be cited the following from a report of the 1st instant made by the Vault, Safe & Lock Expert as a result of his visit to your shops in the latter part of last month.

"They expect to have the vestibules and linings for vaults E and F set up complete for final inspection by the 24th instant and ship same one week later. Those for vaults G and H will follow within three weeks. x x x The six vault doors and one closet door for the minor vaults in the building were being finished in paint shops. These will be ready for shipment by the 5th instant but will be held until vaults E and F are ready."

While it is recognized that you may disclaim responsibility for the statements of the Expert, nevertheless they were based upon what appeared to him to be the conditions and upon the representations made to him while at your shops. Comparing his statements with those made by you about a month later, it seems that you are not making much progress.

Respectfully,

(Signed) J. K. Taylor.

Supervising Architect.

67

DENVER, NEW MINT.

OFFICE OF SUPERVISING ARCHITECT

IN REPLYING, QUOTE UPPER INITIAL, RIGHT HAND CORNER.

TREASURY DEPARTMENT

WASHINGTON April 2, 1904.

Superintendent of Construction,

New Mint Building,

Denver, Colorado.

Sir:-

The Director of the Mint reports to this office that the voucher, in amount $1,600.00, in favor of S. Faith and Company, on account of their work for the mechanical equipment, etc., at the building in your charge, issued and certified by you some time since, and forwarded to the Department for payment from the appropriation for "New Machinery, Mint at Denver", has been lost or mislaid, and has never been paid. A recent voucher carrying a payment to the same firm, in amount $5,600.00, chargeable to the same appropriation, referred to the Director for settlement, with the customary notation of the prior payment of $1,600.00, occasioned the discovery of the fact that the latter amount had not been paid.

In order that the Contractors may have a settlement of the amount due them effected upon a proper basis, it is desired that you will consider the voucher originally issued for $1,600.00 as canceled, and that you will now issue and certify another voucher in an appropriate amount, less the $5,600.00 above referred to as a payment on account, and forward the same to this office for check and transmission to the Director of the Mint, for settlement in the usual and customary manner.

It is suggested, inasmuch as it is understood here that the Superintendent of the Mint occasionally makes disbursements upon the order of the Department, that you confer with that official and ascertain whether by any possibility the payment of $1,600.00 on account, above referred to, could have been made without the Department, in the absence of the receipt of the Superintendent's accounts, being aware of the transaction. Having satisfied yourself that the amount is yet outstanding, you are requested to proceed as suggested above.

Respectfully,

Supervising Architect.

FD

Flour City Ornamental Iron Works
27th Ave. 27th St. & 28th Ave. South
Eugene Tetzlaff, Prest.
Ernest Russert, Vice Prest.
Fredk Schilling, Secy
L. B. Vollmer, Treas.
Minneapolis, Minn.

STRIKES, ACCIDENTS AND OTHER DELAYS UNAVOIDABLE OR BEYOND OUR CONTROL

Apr. 4, '04.

68

Mr. W. E. Ellery,

Supt. New Denver Mint Bldg.,

Denver, Col.

Dear Sir:

We are informed by our men at the building that you have requested us to furnish an iron trimming also, for the door in back of elevator "C" 2. This was originally shown to be iron, and was so detailed by us and submitted to the government's approval, but they changed it to wood trimming, therefore, this was omitted. If this was again to be changed to iron, it would cost considerable trouble and unnecessary expense. If, however, you feel that this ought to be iron and wish to order it so, we shall have to make an extra charge for this.

Awaiting your future commands, we are,

Very truly yours,

FLOUR CITY ORNAMENTAL IRON WORKS

Fred. Schilling

Secy.

Permit No. District No.
Attachment made. 190
To supply premises of

Located in Block , Lot
No. Street
Between Street
and Street.
Plumber.

Location of Stop Box:
ft. from property line on
side of Street ft.
from line of Street.

Location of Tap:
ft. out from side of
Street, ft.
from line of Street.

Description of Premises:
No. Rooms
No. Baths
No. Closets
No. Stores
No. Horses
No. Vehicles
No. Cows
Extras

Denver, Colo. 190

APPLICATION FOR WATER SUPPLY

TO

THE DENVER UNION WATER CO.

I hereby make application for water service to supply my premises No. U S Mint
W Colfax Street,
between Evans and
Sol 13 Street,
Located in Block 10, Lot 1-12
and I hereby agree to abide by all the rules and regulations, and to pay the established rates as made and provided by The Denver Union Water Company.
Signed Frank W. Downer
Remarks: Custodian Mint Building

Duplicate

SEC. 4. All excavations in the streets and alleys of the city must be done in accordance with the ordinance[s and amend]ments of the City Council of the City of Denver or other municipalities where excavations are to be made.
SEC. 5. No street shall be opened, or water pipe tapped, or service pipe be laid down, without written pe[rmission, and] then only by persons authorized by the Water Company, and the particular person to be employed must, in [all cases, be] named in the permit. The ferrule inserted in the distributing main and the service pipe to be laid must be of [the size speci]fied in the permit.
SEC. 6. The tapping of mains shall be under the exclusive control of the Company, and the size of [the ferrule] inserted shall in all cases be determined by the manager of the Company.
SEC. 7. No alteration, addition or disconnection of any fixture, in or about any conduit, pipe or water co[urse or appara]tus connected therewith, shall be made, or cause to be made, by any plumber, for any person taking water, or f[or any purpose] whatsoever, without notice thereof being previously given to, and written permission granted by the Company.
SEC. 8. Any violation of Section 7 will render the plumber liable to a fine of not less than $5 for eac[h fixture] or fixture connected, and the water rates upon the same from the time such connection was made, according [to the Com]pany's schedule.
SEC. 9. Notice must be left at the office of the Company by the plumber about to lay down a service pipe, [...] on which he wishes the tap made. Such notice must be given at least twenty-four hours previous to the time [the exca]vation is begun.
SEC. 10. All service pipes must be of lead, and not less in weight than that called "extra strong."
SEC. 11. All service pipes must be laid at least five feet below the established grade of the streets, and [at] least five feet below the surface of the ground.
SEC. 12. A stop cock, with a round water way, shall be inserted in each service pipe in every case, and a box (to be supplied by the Company, at the expense of the owner of the premises), with a cast iron cover hav[ing] "Denver Union Water Co." thereon; the box shall be placed by the plumber on the edge of the sidewalk, near [...] top even with the pavement and visible.
SEC. 13. When more than one building is supplied by a single tap, by means of branch service pipes, eac[h] must have a stop cock, with like box and cover complete, to be located on the sidewalk in like manner as [...] Section 11.
SEC. 14. Every service pipe shall have a brass top and waste cock, placed within the cellar wall of the b[uilding] accessible to the occupant, so that the water may be drained from the pipes in the house by the occupant, [...] freezing and bursting of pipes; the use of said stop and waste cock must be fully explained to occupants by p[...] the work.
SEC. 15. No hydrant, goose neck, hose bib or faucet shall be located outside the premises for which a lice[nse ...] nor in any open area, or place accessible from adjoining premises; nor over any slop sink or sewer connection.
SEC. 16. Water closets, vaults and urinals must be supplied with self-closing valves, that close with the [...] in no case will a bib or a faucet be allowed to be placed over a closet or urinal.
SEC. 17. *No plumber shall leave the water on after completing the plumbing.*
SEC. 18. Private mains shall not be laid in advance of or beyond the terminus of the Company's pipes, [...] option of the Company.
SEC. 19. A street wa[...] will not be allowed on the sidewalk, except where the building is set out to the street line, thus leaving no room for it [...] the lot.
SEC. 20. Where service pipes are found disconnected at the corporation cock or main, they may be reconnected only by the Company.
SEC. 21. All outlets in service pipes must be provided with air chambers not less than 18 inches on the first floor and 12 inches on upper floors. All air chambers must be securely capped.
SEC. 22. Corporation cocks will be furnished and taps made by the Company at the following prices:

For ½ inch Corporation Cock and Tapping	$2.00	For ¾ inch Corporation Cock and Tapping	$5.00
For ⅝ inch Corporation Cock and Tapping	3.00	For 1 inch Corporation Cock and Tapping	6.00
For ¾ inch Corporation Cock and Tapping	4.00	Stop Box and Water Way	2.50

SEC. 23. Any violation of any of the above rules by any plumber, shall be deemed a breach of the condition of his bond.

THE DENVER UNION WATER COMPANY.

DENVER, NEW MINT.

OFFICE OF SUPERVISING ARCHITECT

IN REPLYING, QUOTE UPPER INITIAL, RIGHT HAND CORNER.

70

TREASURY DEPARTMENT

WASHINGTON April 2, 1904.

Inclosure No. 1165.

Superintendent of Construction,
New Mint Building,
Denver, Colo.

Sir:-

There is inclosed herewith, for your information and the files of your office, copy of letter of even date, approving samples of hardware submitted by the contractor for the completion of the building in your charge, and the approved samples are forwarded, under separate cover, for the files of your office and your guidance in accepting the work.

Respectfully,

J. K. Taylor
Supervising Architect.

KCH

DENVER, NEW MINT.

April 2, 1904.

Mr. James A. McGonigle,

Leavenworth, Kansas.

Sir:-

I have to acknowledge receipt of your letter of the 27th ultimo, and, under separate cover, the samples referred to therein, submitted for approval in connection with your contract for the completion of the New Mint building at Denver, Colorado, and you are advised that the following, as represented by such samples are approved for use wherever materials of the character represented thereby are required in the work:

Composition metal sash chain,
Sash balance,
Cabinet lock,
Sash hook,
Spring catch,
Lever latch and handles,
Ring sash catch,
Door hook,
Sash stay chain,

The steel sash chain is not approved as it does not appear that such material is required.

In the above approval, where appliances are intended to perform special service, as for instance, sash balance, the approval is for mechanism only and appliances furnished must be capable of doing the work.

Respectfully,

Supervising Architect.

[illegible] [illegible] Construction, Mint [illegible]

[illegible] 19[illegible]

[illegible] M. [illegible]owner, Assayer in Charge, [illegible]

[illegible] and Custodian of the [illegible] Mint

[illegible] instructed to assume the duties

[illegible] [illegible] directed to transfer

all [illegible], [illegible], and [illegible]

[illegible] [illegible]

[illegible] thereof [illegible] be forwarded [illegible]

[illegible] file.

Respectfully,

DENVER, NEW MINT.

OFFICE OF SUPERVISING ARCHITECT

IN REPLYING QUOTE UPPER INITIAL, RIGHT HAND CORNER.

92

TREASURY DEPARTMENT

WASHINGTON April 5, 1904.

Inclosure No. 1168.

Superintendent of Construction,
New Mint Building,
Denver, Colorado.

Sir:-

There is inclosed herewith, for your information and the files of your office, copy of Department letter of even date, accepting the proposal of Messrs. S. Faith & Company, to substitute gauges manufactured by the American Steam Gauge and Valve Company, in lieu of those manufactured by the Star Brass Manufacturing Company as specified in their contract for the mechanical equipment of the building in your charge, without expense to the Government.

Respectfully,

J. K. Taylor
Supervising Architect.

KCH

DENVER, NEW MINT.

April 8, 1904.

Messrs. S. Faith & Co.,
New Mint Building,
Denver, Colo.

Gentlemen:-

Your proposal of March 31, 1904, to substitute gauges manufactured by the American Steam Gauge and Valve Company, in lieu of those manufactured by the Star Brass Manufacturing Company as specified in your contract for the mechanical equipment of the New Mint building at Denver, Colorado, without expense, is accepted, it being understood that such change is not to relieve you from furnishing gauges in all respects as required in the specification, a public exigency requiring this change in the contract.

It is understood and agreed that this acceptance is not to affect the time for the completion of the entire work as required by the terms of your contract; that the same is without prejudice to any and all rights of the United States thereunder; and without prejudice, also, to any and all rights of the United States against the sureties on the bond executed for the faithful fulfillment of the contract.

Please promptly acknowledge the receipt of this letter, a copy of which has been forwarded to the Superintendent.

Respectfully,

Assistant Secretary.

J.C.P.
KCM

[illegible]

Respectfully,

[illegible]

DENVER NEW MINT. Cross file HELENA, MONT., P.O. 74

OFFICE OF SUPERVISING ARCHITECT

IN REPLYING QUOTE UPPER INITIAL RIGHT HAND CORNER

TREASURY DEPARTMENT S

WASHINGTON April 6, 1904.

Enclosure 18.

Mr. Lee Ullery,
Superintendent of Construction,
New Mint,
Denver, Colorado.

Sir:

Referring to telegram of this date, enclosed find Department letter of the 5th instant, transferring you for duty, incident to the completion of the U. S. Public Building, at Helena, Montana, to take effect on the 16th instant, with compensation reduced to $2,190.00 per annum.

You are requested to leave for your new duties, at Helena, Montana, on the 16th instant, and on the 15th instant, to forward to this office, a complete report, in line with Section XL of printed "Instructions to Superintendents", giving the conditions of the work under the various contracts at the Denver New Mint, itemizing all defects, omissions and uncompleted work.

Mr. A. A. Packard, Inspector of Public Buildings, owing to the death of the late Superintendent of Construction, at the Helena, building, is temporarily in charge, and he will be informed of your coming.

Mr. B. H. Tatem, U. S. Assayor at Helena, has been directed to assume temporary custody of the building and its contents, and he will also be informed of your detail, with the request that he transfer the property to your charge upon your arrival.

Please wire the date of your arrival at Helena.

Respectfully,

Supervising Architect.

DENVER MINT (NEW).

MGD

OFFICE OF SUPERVISING ARCHITECT

IN REPLYING, QUOTE UPPER INITIAL, RIGHT HAND CORNER.

FORWARDING EXP.
ENCLOSURE 1926.

7 / d

TREASURY DEPARTMENT FBU

WASHINGTON April 6, 1904.

The Superintendent of Construction,

U. S. Mint (New),

Denver, Col.

Sir:

For your information find herewith copy of office letter of this date, addressed to C. Faith and Company, contractors for mechanical equipment of the building for which you are Superintendent, advising them of approval of Howard hose rack (Figure 8) and unlined linen hose, both as per samples submitted, which are forwarded to you to-day, by express, charges prepaid.

Respectfully,

L.

J. K. Taylor
Supervising Architect.

DENVER MINT (NEW).

MGD

April 6, 1904.

Messrs. S. Faith and Company,

#2427 Pennsylvania Avenue,

F

Philadelphia, Pa.

Sirs:

Referring to your contract for mechanical equipment of the U. S. Mint (new), Denver, Col., receipt is acknowledged of your letter of the 24th ultimo, submitting sample hose rack (H. J. M. Howard, Figure 8) which you desire to use in lieu of the Nuhring rack formerly submitted, and rejected by this office.

The Howard rack is now approved, as is also the sample of unlined linen hose submitted, and both will be sent to the Superintendent of Construction at the building.

Respectfully,

(Signed) J.K.Taylor

Supervising Architect.

L CEK

DENVER, NEW MINT.

/

TREASURY DEPARTMENT

WASHINGTON April 9, 1904

IN REPLYING, QUOTE UPPER INITIAL, RIGHT HAND CORNER

Inclosure No. 1187.

Superintendent of Construction,
New Mint Building,
Denver, Colorado.

Sir:-

There is inclosed herewith, for your information and the files of your office, copy of letter of even date, requesting proposal from the contractors for the mechanical equipment of the building in your charge, to substitute instruments made by the Western Electrical Company for those required by their contract.

Respectfully,

J K Taylor
Supervising Architect.

KCH

DENVER, NEW MINT.

April 9, 1904.

Messrs. E. Faith & Company,
New Mint Building,
Denver, Colorado.

Gentlemen:-

Referring to your contract for the mechanical equipment of the New Mint building at Denver, Colorado, and to the Keystone instruments included therein, for use upon the switchboard, it is understood that no work has been done towards making these instruments, and you are requested to forward a proposal for installing instruments made by the Western Electrical Company in lieu of those required by the contract; such proposal to be in two items, one for the total amount for making the change and one stating amount included for instruments on panel marked "C", drawing N.V.-28.

It is requested that this matter receive very prompt attention, and upon receipt of such proposal prompt action will be taken.

Respectfully,

Supervising Architect.

KCW

[illegible]

DIEBOLD SAFE AND LOCK CO.

SAFES **LOCKS**

April 6, 1904,

Mr. Lee Ulery,
Supt. Denver Mint Bldg.,
Denver, Colo.

Dear Sir:-

With reference to the Fire-proof vestibules and doors we are furnishing for the Denver Mint Bldg. we wish to ascertain if it will be necessary to ship these doors in advance of Vaults B, F, G. & N.? We have written the Supervising Architect that these will be shipped in fifteen to eighteen days, and if necessary we will ship these Fire-proof doors in advance, as they are in the paint [illegible] and can be shipped at any time.

Please advise, and oblige.

Yours respectfully,

[illegible] Presd.

79

Printed Heading.

Philadelphia, April 11,1904.

Mr.Lee Ullery,

Supt. of Construction,

U.S.Mint Building, Denver, Colorado.

Dear Sir:-

We will furnish and put in place a 2 inch conduit (similar to other conduits under our contract for the building under your charge) run from behind the switchboard in engine room,beneath floors through walls and into the sweeps room, to be constructed outside and at the southwest corner of the building. The conduit to be carried up in the corner to the spring of the arch, all as indicated on drawing No.247-A, all for the sum of EIGHTY SEVEN DOLLARS($87.oo).

(Signed) S.Faith & Company,
S.

DENVER (new) MINT.

80

TREASURY DEPARTMENT FBW

WASHINGTON April 13, 1904.

The Superintendent of Construction,

United States New Mint,

Denver, Colorado.

Sir:

The receipt of your letter of the 7th instant relative to the trim of door C-11, to be supplied under the contract for the interior finish of the building for which you are the Superintendent of Construction, is hereby acknowledged.

In reply you are informed that approved shop drawing No. E-3, modified by pencil note quoted, is to govern, this being done that the finish may be as uniform as possible.

Respectfully,

J. K. Taylor
Supervising Architect.

R.

[illegible]

[illegible], [illegible] ADDRESS SUPERINTENDENT OF REMITTANCE [illegible]

Treasury Department.

[illegible]

Washington, D. C., April [illegible] 19[illegible].

Superintendent of Construction,

Mint Building, Denver, Colo.

Sir:

The Estimate of funds required during the month of April [illegible], for the work under your charge has been received, and you are advised that a remittance of $50,000.00 to the Disbursing Agent has been requested.

Respectfully,

[illegible signature]

Chief Executive Officer.

DENVER, NEW MINT.

OFFICE OF SUPERVISING ARCHITECT

IN REPLYING QUOTE UPPER INITIAL, RIGHT HAND CORNER.

82

TREASURY DEPARTMENT

WASHINGTON April 14, 1904.

Inclosure No. 459.

Superintendent of Construction,
New Mint Building,
Denver, Colo.

Sir:-

There is inclosed herewith, for your information and the files of your office, copy of Department letter of even date, accepting the proposal of S. Faith & Company, in amount twenty dollars ($20.00), to place a 4" cast iron drain pipe to drain the scale pit indicated on drawing No. P-73, as an addition to their contract for the mechanical equipment of the building in your charge; and you are hereby authorized to certify and issue vouchers on account of the work, as required by the terms of the contract and in accordance with the printed "Instructions to Superintendents", payment of which vouchers the Disbursing Agent has this day been authorized to make from the appropriation for New Mint, Denver, Colorado.

Respectfully,

J K Taylor
Supervising Architect.

KCH

DENVER, NEW MINT.

April 14, 1904.

Messrs. J. . ith & Company,
New Mint Building,
Denver, Colo.

Gentlemen:-

In view of the statements and recommendation contained in letter of the 7th instant, from the Superintendent of Construction for the New Mint building at Denver, Colorado, your proposal of the 7th instant, in amount twenty dollars ($20.00), is accepted to place a 4" cast iron drain pipe to drain the scale pit indicated on drawing No. P-73, as directed by the Superintendent and to his full satisfaction, the amount being deemed reasonable and a public exigency requiring the performance of the work, which is to be considered as an addition to your contract for the mechanical equipment of the building.

It is understood and agreed that this acceptance is not to affect the time for the completion of the entire work as required by the terms of your contract, that the same is without prejudice to any and all rights of the United States thereunder; and without prejudice, also, to any and all rights of the United States against the sureties on the bond executed for the faithful fulfillment of the contract.

Please promptly acknowledge the receipt of this letter, a copy of which is forwarded to the Superintendent.

Respectfully,

J.C.P.
KCW

Assistant Secretary.

83

DENVER MINT (NEW).

MCD

IN REPLYING, QUOTE UPPER INITIAL, RIGHT HAND CORNER.

ENCLOSURE 1947.
FORWARDING.EXP.

TREASURY DEPARTMENT FBW

WASHINGTON April 14, 1904.

The Superintendent of Construction,

U. S. Mint (New),

Denver, Col.

Sir:

Referring to a contract with Messrs. S. Faith and Company, for mechanical equipment of the building for which you are the Superintendent of Construction, find herewith copy of office letter of this date, addressed to the contractors named, advising them of approval of sample self-closing lavatory faucet, which will be sent to you to-day, by express, charges prepaid.

Please note the modification in regard to couplings.

Respectfully,

J. K. Taylor
Supervising Architect.

April 14, 1904.

Messrs. S. Faith and Company,

#2427 Pennsylvania Avenue,

B

Philadelphia, Pa.

Sirs:

Referring to your contract for mechanical equipment of the U. S. Mint (new), Denver, Col., receipt is acknowledged of your letter of the 12th instant, forwarding self-closing lavatory faucet, and you are advised that same is approved; with the understanding, however, that faucets furnished must be fitted with couplings for screw-jointed connections, instead of coupling for soldered connection to lead pipe, as per sample.

The sample faucet will be sent to the Superintendent, with copy of this letter.

Respectfully,

(Signed) J.K.Taylor,
Supervising Architect.

L CEK

Superintendent of Construction,
New Mint Building,
Denver, Colorado.

Sir:-

I have to acknowledge receipt of your letter [illegible]
instant, relative to painting copper work at the ce
in second story and ceiling of transfer room and sc
in first story, and you are directed to have the co
without painting, inasmuch as painting is not requ
contract.

Respectfully,

[illegible]
Sup'vis'g [illegible]

[illegible]

[illegible] DEPARTMENT [illegible]

[illegible]

[illegible], April [illegible] 19[illegible]

R

Mr. [illegible]

Superintendent of Construction [illegible]

[illegible]

Sir:

[illegible]

[illegible]

[illegible] and detailing you for duty on the [illegible] Building [illegible] taking effect April 25, 19[illegible], and [illegible] your compensation from the rate of $[illegible] per annum to the rate of $[illegible] per annum during such detail. [illegible] and your [illegible] of the [illegible], [illegible] compensation [illegible] rate of $[illegible] per annum from April [illegible], 19[illegible].

You are [illegible] for [illegible].

Respectfully,

[illegible]

88

TREASURY DEPARTMENT

OFFICE OF THE SECRETARY

WASHINGTON, April 18, 1904.

Mr. Lee Ullery,

Superintendent of Construction, Mint Building,

Denver, Colo.

Sir:

Department letter of April 4, 1904, directing you to transfer the custody of the U. S. Mint Building, Denver, Colo., to Frank M. Downer, Assayer in Charge, U. S. Mint, on April 15, 1904, is hereby revoked.

Respectfully,

Secretary.

C. L.
T.

DENVER MINT, NEW.

April 19, 1904.

(MCGONIGLE # [illegible])

The Superintendent of Construction,

U. S. Mint Building,

Denver, Colorado

Sir:

There is enclosed herewith for information and file a copy of Office letter this day addressed to Mr. James A. McGonigle, together with one print each of shop drawings Nos. 270 and 271, therein mentioned, showing doors, grilles, etc., for the Money Storage Room in connection with the building for which you are the Superintendent of Construction.

Respectfully,

Supervising Architect

DENVER MINT, NEW.

April 1[illegible],1904.

(ENCLOSURE [illegible])

Mr. James A. McGonigle,

New Mint Building,

Denver, Colorado.

Sir:

The Office is in receipt of your communication of April 1[illegible]th, transmitting, in quadruplicate, shop drawings for doors, grilles, etc., in connection with [illegible] Storage Room, new U.S. Mint Building, Denver, Colorado, and in reply you are informed that said drawings have been given Office numbers 870 and 871, and two sets of the prints are herewith returned, approved as to general construction.

Respectfully,

Supervising Architect.

D.

The Superintendent of Construction
Mint Building (New),
Denver, Colorado.

Sirs:

In view of the statement and recommendation contained in your letter of the 30th ultimo, you are hereby authorized to accept the following proposals, copies enclosed, for the purchase of the old materials at the building under your charge, the same being the highest bids he could obtain, the old materials to be removed at once from the premises.

I. Goldstein,		
fence around site,	$ [illegible]	
stone flagging	1[illegible]	
cast iron pipe etc.,	1[illegible]	
scrap iron etc.,	[illegible]	$ [illegible]
G. W. [illegible],		
Superintendent's office building	$ [illegible]	[illegible]
Hyman Lifshitz,		
manhole cap stones and cast iron covers	$ 5.00	5.00

Please secure payment of the purchase money before removal of the old materials, and deposit the proceeds of the sales with the nearest United States depository to the credit of the Treasurer of the United States on account of "Proceeds for sale of miscellaneous materials."

In the event that the highest bidder, in any case, fails to carry into effect his proposal in accordance with specifications on file in your office, the amount of proceeds of certified checks will be forfeited, and you are requested to advise the office of the Supervising Architect thereof in order that consideration may be gi to acceptance of the next highest bid in any given case. In this connection you are also advised that the certified checks submitted by all bidders will be held until receipt of information from you in regard to the above.

Respectfully,

[signature]

Acting Secretary.

EXTRACT COPY:

PROPOSAL FOR OFFICE BUILDING AND OTHER PROPERTY AT THE
U.S. MINT BUILDING, DENVER, COLORADO.

Denver, Colo.March 30,1904.

Superintendent of Construction,
Mint Building, Denver, Colorado.

Sir:-

I hereby propose to pay for the U.S.property offered for sale, the following amounts:-

* *

For fence enclosing site--------------------------$70.00

For stone flagging-------------------------------$155.00

For cast iron soil pipe and cleanout frames and covers------------------------------$148.00

For the wrough iron grilles and beams, channels,etc.,-------------------------------$65.00

* *

(Signed) D.Goldstein,

(Address) 1240 Larner St.

EXTRACT COPY:

PROPOSAL FOR OFFICE BUILDING AND OTHER PROPERTY AT THE
U.S.MINT BUILDING, DENVER, COLORADO.

Denver, Colo.,March 28, 1904.

Superintendent of Construction,

Mint Building, Denver,Colorado.

Sir:-

______ hereby propose to pay for the U.S.property offered for sale, the following amounts:-

* *

For the manhole cap stones and cast iron covers for same-----------------------------$5.00.

* *

(Signature) Hyman Lifshitz..

(Address) 1336 Evans st.,

Denver,Colo.

91

Address all communications to the Company

The Denver Iron & Wire Works Co

STRUCTURAL AND ORNAMENTAL IRON AND STEEL

All agreements subject to strikes, accidents or other causes beyond our control

1401-3-5-7 Market Street

Denver, Colorado, Apr. 28, 1904.

Mr. Ullery, Supt.,

U. S. Mint,

Denver.

Dear Sir:-

In line with our conversation over the 'Phone this morning, regarding elevator enclosures for Cheyenne Post Office. As requested by you we will proceed with the assembling of grille work for these elevator enclosures with the understanding that if any additional material or labor is required, by the supervising architect, to stiffen the bars, same will be applied after grille work is assembled; and if this is necessary we will be advised through the Cheyenne contractors, Messrs. Forster & Smith.

Yours truly,

J.J

THE DENVER IRON & WIRE WORKS CO.

DENVER NEW MINT.

OFFICE OF SUPERVISING ARCHITECT

IN REPLYING, QUOTE UPPER INITIAL, RIGHT HAND CORNER.

92

TREASURY DEPARTMENT

WASHINGTON April 23, 1904.

Enclosure 37.

Superintendent of Construction,
U. S. Mint (New),
Denver, Colorado.

Sir:

Enclosed find copy of a report, dated the 18th instant, as the result of an examination of work under the contract for the mechanical equipment, &c., of the building under your charge.

Respectfully,

L
Jas

J. K. Taylor
Supervising Architect.

Construction,

Mint Building,

Denver, Colo., April 18,1904.

The Supervising Architect,

Treasury Department, Washington, D.C.

Sir:-

In compliance with Department instructions of April 2nd,1904(initial F.S.W.),I have visited the United States Mint (new) at Denver,Colorado,and have made an examination of the work installed to date in connection with the Mechanical Equipment(except engines and generators)under contract with S.Faith & Co. of Philadelphia,Pa.

I also made investigation as to the delay being caused by this and other contracts,and the general prospects of more vigorous action on the part of the contractors and the early completion of the work.

The mechanical equipment work has undoubtedly been the cause of delay of certain parts of the general contract,and is still preventing work being done in some directions; but the work delayed at present need not cause delay in completion of the building,if materials arrive promptly and the work is pushed.

While the general contract work prevents to a limited extent completion of the mechanical equipment in certain particulars,these delays will not affect materially the time of final completion of the latter contract.

The delay in receipt of boilers(only two being yet at the building), and in receipt of the indirect heaters and air supply fans has prevented [illegible] work in the basement being done, and this, and the failure of the [illegible] authorities making inspection of all tanks in delaying some work of the contractor. The delay in receipt of ventilating fans has caused [illegible] parts of the attic to be left unfinished for the present.

The marble work under both the general contract and mechanical equipment contract has caused delays to both of said contracts. This work for both contracts is under the same sub-contractor, and while considerable marble is now on hand, and being set, other work in both contracts is being delayed. The marble has been slow both in shipment and in transit, and has been shipped in such manner as to prevent the completion of the work at any one point, and just now an insufficient number of marble setters are available.

I can state, however, that at this time conditions have improved in every way under both contracts, and that there is every indication that the work throughout will now progress rapidly and harmoniously until completion.

The work that has been executed under the mechanical equipment contract has been done in accordance with the contract, except in a few instances which were called to my attention by the Superintendent and in [illegible], and the Superintendent is now having the corrections made and making adjustment of the necessary deviations. These items are as follows.

their place.

2. Some of the vent ducts have wide surfaces that are not braced with angle irons; this bracing will be placed.

3. Drip pipe from exhaust head above roof has been omitted; this will be put in and connected to drip from bottom of exhaust pipe.

4. The economizer is constructed and set so that connections cannot be made to permit of one half being used for heating house water, and to attempt to make changes to accomplish this result would cause objectionable conditions in other respects; so I recommend that the economizer remain as at present and have connections made so that it can be used for either heating feed water or for heating house water, the entire economizer being used for one purpose at a time. The Superintendent will obtain proposals for this change and forward.

5. Some of the old cast iron drain pipe removed from the first system, the property of the Government, has been used for pipe sleeves in the wall; the Superintendent will obtain a proposal for deduction on this account and forward.

6. The conduit, wire and junction boxes at outside standards have been omitted from the general contract, and the conduit and wire of mechanical equipment contract has been extended from location of junction boxes up into the standards; this change is an improvement and the contractors have been requested by the Superintendent to submit proposals for the changes which will be forwarded when received.

----------M---------

The general condition of work under the various sections of the mechanical equipment contract is as follows.

SECTION I. Plumbing and Gas Piping and Finish of Toilet Rooms.

All cast iron, wrought iron, earthenware and lead lined drain, soil, waste, vent, water, fire and gas pipes are roughed in complete, except as to a few very minor matters.

The catch basins, cesspools, floor drains and the waste water tanks and covers are in place complete.

Wall hydrants and hose connections are in place.

The marble work of toilet rooms is now about 75% complete, together with about the same proportion of nickel plated brasses, etc.

A few of the plumbing fixtures in basement and large attic toilet rooms have been set, but generally are not connected to the water and waste piping.

Toilet room floors where terrazzo is called for have not been laid, but the cement floors in basement and attic toilet rooms are in place.

Woodwork under plumbing has not been placed.

Registers in toilet rooms and vent grate marble is in place.

The marble work and flooring of toilet rooms is expected to be completed very soon, which will be followed immediately with the setting and connecting of fixtures and placing of woodwork. All the plumbing fixtures except stone sinks and wash basins are now on hand.

This section of the work is estimated to be 90% completed.

SECTION II. Steam Power Plant, &c.

The high pressure steam drum is now being erected and the small low pressure and practically all the medium pressure steam piping is in place. The main exhaust pipe is in place from heater to roof with exhaust head also in place, and exhaust pipe is in place from draft fan engine. Practically no drain piping and very little drip piping is installed. No blow off piping is in place, but the vapor pipes from blow-off tank and drip tank are in place to roof. The water piping under this section of the specification has not been run.

Two of the steam boilers are now in the building and being erected, the columns, girders and foundations for these two being in place. Portions of the other two boilers are now being delivered at the building, and the remaining portions have been shipped. A member of the contracting firm, who is now here, states that the trouble and delay in getting the boilers was caused by the failure of boiler manufacturer, making it necessary to take action through the courts to secure possession of and to complete the boilers. The Hawley furnaces are not yet at the building, but reported to be in transit. Boiler fronts not yet received at the building.

The smoke stack and smoke header are in place, but the breeching cannot be placed until boiler settings are started. The draft fan and its engine are in place, complete, and connected to smoke header and to the [illegible]ine.

The economizer is in place complete, except the operating motor. The motor is at the building. As previously stated, the connections to economizer will have to be made differently from what is shown [illegible] detailed, proposals for which will be forwarded by the Superintendent.

The platform over smoke header, etc., coal scales, boiler trimmings, etc cannot be placed until other work is further advanced. The ash hoist is in place and practically complete, except the placing and connecting of motor. The motor is at the building.

The boiler feed pumps are set up complete and connected, except to the exhaust and drip mains. The two house pumps are set on their foundations, but the motors are not yet set and no piping is in place. The air compressors are ready to be placed on their foundations.

The pressure tank for house water supply and the air storage tank are in place on their foundations, but no connections made therefrom. The fresh water storage tank is not built, though arrangements are now being made for its construction, as the artesian well is now completed to its proper depth.

The drip tank is in place complete, except its cover, which is ready to place. The centrifugal pump and motor for drip tank are not yet at the building. The blow-off tank is in place and connection therefrom made to sewer and to vapor pipe.

The medium pressure separators are in place and the high pressure separators will be placed when their steam main is erected. The pressure reducing valves and the back pressure valves are in place, but drip pot is not in place, and no steam traps or drips are in place.

The open feed water heater is in place and partly connected. The hot water storage heater is not in place, or at the building.

The pipe trenches under this section are only partly formed and the iron work of same is not placed and cannot be set or the trenches completed until other work is further advanced.

This section of the work is now coming along very well, and the appliances and auxiliaries are being received and the work generally is being pushed.

The estimated amount of work under this section now in place is [illegible] %.

SECTION VII. Heating and Ventilating Apparatus.

The Webster Vacuum System has been approved for this work, and the pumps therefor are set on their foundations, but no connections made thereto.

All the low pressure steam piping is in place except connections for the air heating coils, and all return piping above the basement is in place complete.

The direct radiators are all in the building, and, except in a few instances, are connected up in their permanent positions. The indirect or air heating coils are not on hand, but are reported to be in transit. [illegible] fans and motors.

The pipe trenches with their cover plates are generally in place where called for under this section, and a small amount of the cover plates are in place but not finally fitted.

The air filters, [illegible] fan, suction and fresh chamber dampers, etc., have not been placed or any work done in the building in connection therewith.

None of the disc fans, the exhauster or their motors are at the building, but they are expected shortly, having been shipped about the 1st instant.

All galvanized iron air and vent ducts are in place, except some ward

...ions fan chambers and at entrance to the

...rs, some additional bracing of ducts has

...til fume pipe ducts are in place.

...portion of the work is as far advanced as

...f heater coils, fans, etc., and upon their ...

...event the rapid prosecution of the work, wh...

All the cabinets for distribution centers are in place, and the cabinets for same are at the building together with most of the frames for same.

All outlets and boxes are in place for telephone, clock and fire alarm systems, and also other special conduits called for.

The work is as far advanced as is possible and has caused very little and is now causing no delay whatever in the other work.

It is estimated that 80% of this section of the work is completed.

SECTION VI. Electric Elevators.

The three elevators machines are in place complete, and also the overhead work.

The guides are complete in one shaft, but not commenced in the other two shafts.

The elevator cages and cars are not at the building.

All the cables for this work are at the building, and a sample has been sent to the office for analysis to determine as to its complying with the specification before same are strung.

This work is well advanced and there is nothing to prevent its early completion, the estimated amount now completed is 80%.

SECTION VII. Non Conducting Coverings

No non-conducting coverings have been placed, and no approved samples have been received at the building.

The contractor for mechanical equipment realizes the importance of [illegible]ing Architect [illegible]

[illegible] work, and the [illegible] important appliances and materials [illegible] in the building [illegible] in progress, I see no reason why [illegible] be completed in a reasonably short time and [illegible] to work under the general [illegible]

Respectfully submitted,

[illegible]

Assistant Chief Mechanical and Electrical Engineer.

Denver, Colorado [illegible]

April [illegible]

R. Bernard [illegible]

Ass't. Chief Mechanical and
Electrical Engineer.

Report [illegible] and investigation of the [illegible]
[illegible] for Mechanical Equipment
[illegible] engines and generators
for the United States Mint Building, Denver, Colorado.

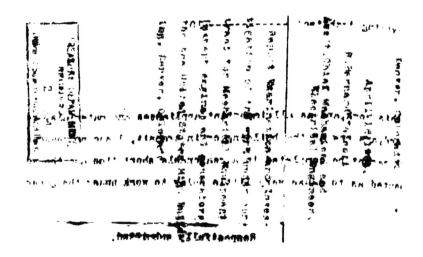

TREASURY DEPARTMENT
RECEIVED
2 [illegible]
Office Supervising Architect

ENTER NEW MINT.

Inclosure 656.

TREASURY DEPARTMENT

WASHINGTON April 27, 1904.

Superintendent of Construction,
New Mint Building,
Denver, Colorado.

Sir:

I inclose herewith, for your information and the files of your office, a copy of Department letter of even date, accepting the proposal of S. Faith & Company, in amount eighty-seven dollars ($87.00), as an addition to their contract for the mechanical equipment of the building in your charge, to furnish and place a 2" conduit from back of switchboard in engine room into the sweeps room; and you are hereby authorized to certify and issue vouchers for the work, as required by the terms of the contract and the printed "Instructions to Superintendents", payment of which vouchers the Disbursing Agent has been authorized to make from the appropriation for Mint Building, Denver, Colorado.

Respectfully,

JSS

Supervising Architect.

[illegible] & Co.,
[illegible] Pennsylvania Avenue,
Philadelphia, Pa.

Gentlemen;

In view of the statement and recommendation contained in letter of the 16th instant, from the Superintendent of Construction of the New Mint Building, Denver, Colorado, your proposal, dated the 11th instant, addressed to him, in amount eighty-seven dollars ($87.00), is hereby accepted, as an addition to your contract for the mechanical equipment of the building, to furnish and place a 4" conduit from back of switchboard in engine room, into the [illegible] room, in accordance with the terms of your proposal, and to the satisfaction of the Superintendent, a public exigency requiring the immediate performance of the work.

It is understood and agreed that this acceptance is not to affect the time for the completion of the work as required by the terms of your contract; that the same is without prejudice to any and all rights of the United States thereunder; and without prejudice, also, to any and all rights of the United States against the sureties on the bond executed for the faithful fulfillment of the contract.

Please acknowledge the receipt of this letter.

Respectfully,

Acting Secretary.

T.
J.C.P.
JSS

DENVER (NEW MINT).

MGD

April 26, 1904.

Messrs. S. Faith and Company,

P #2427 Pennsylvania Avenue,

Philadelphia, Pa.

Sirs:

Referring to your contract for mechanical equipment of the U. S. Mint (New), Denver, Col., and especially to elevator work included in same, you are advised that a sample cut from the elevator hoisting cables delivered at the building has been tested in the laboratory of this office, and found to be steel, instead of Swedish iron required by the specification.

Said cables are therefore rejected, and must be removed from the premises, and in lieu thereof you must furnish cables fully in accordance with specification requirements.

Copy of this letter will be sent to the Superintendent of Construction.

Respectfully,

(Signed) J.K.Taylor

Supervising Architect.

L CEK

Denver Mint.

Cleveland, Ohio, April 25, 1904.

The Supervising Architect,

Treasury Department,

Washington, D.C.

Dear Sir:-

On instructions dated the 16th inst. I visited the works of the Diebold Safe & Lock Co. on the 18th inst. and remained there for the succeeding four days, making careful inspection of the vault work for the mint at Denver, Col.

Reports, except the mass of the details, developed from day to day, could not be made there, as the vital question of whether there would be objection to the shipment was not determined until evening of the 5th day, too late for a summary to be properly presented without losing the business hours of the next day and it is handed you herewith.

The four smaller vestibules were standing and attached to their linings. The work of hot riveting the lining connections, with pneumatic machines and hand hammers where necessary was progressing. Three sets of outer and inner doors, with all bolt work, lever, and hinge attachements, were hung in places and the work of finally fitting them to the jambs begun. The outer doors were fitted perfectly before I left. A different set of workmen had the inner doors to do and both sets could not work at the same time, so that but one inner door set was completed. The smallest clearance between inner doors found was 43-3/4".

The moveable thresholds were complete in themselves. They must be fitted to the floor beams, etc. at the building.

[illegible] were [illegible] the same. One of them was [illegible]

[illegible]

[illegible] separate [illegible]

[illegible] Bureau [illegible]

[illegible] the [illegible]

[illegible] would [illegible] the [illegible]

[illegible] projections required and [illegible]

[illegible] with each one to separate them. [illegible]

[illegible] of [illegible]

[illegible]

[illegible] course of the [illegible] was [illegible]

[illegible] occurred at the [illegible]

[illegible] the upper entrance to the [illegible] was

[illegible] the [illegible]

[illegible] of the [illegible]

[illegible] would strike the [illegible]

[illegible] the [illegible] projection [illegible]

[illegible] that the [illegible]

[illegible]

[illegible] would have too much [illegible] with the

[illegible] for the lock. I ordered the gates to [illegible]

[illegible] will [illegible] these changes

without extra charge. It will leave the [illegible]

[illegible] were [illegible] and [illegible]

[illegible] of low wheel trucks [illegible] ordered the

A[illegible] other details of the work were found to be as shown [illegible] approved prints and as specified for.

The [illegible] linings were to be taken down, refitted again, [illegible] their vestibules, shipped in [illegible] working days, the fifth [illegible] will be held for final adjustment of all work, etc. and with the gates follow in twenty days, [illegible] the time the rough work is assembled in place.

Work is progressing rapidly on the [illegible] vault. Except [illegible] has been previously reported as to stiffening of the [illegible], no changes were found necessary. [illegible] of [illegible] employed on it and it is expected to ship the [illegible] parts [illegible] in place within four weeks from April 26, or the 26th

The six vault doors and one closet door for the [illegible] are to be forwarded with the first shipment. They have been [illegible] some time.

No one at the shops doubt that the entire work will [illegible] by July 15th next. Each of the five vault sets is [illegible] of many workmen from the various departments, each assembling [illegible] details into the completed whole, very often in such [illegible] way. Had the same diligence been possible when the con[illegible] was let, the work would have been completed six months

... will be.

... ectfully submitted,

[illegible]

... & ... Gilbert.

PRINTED HEADING.

Philadelphia, April 26,1904.

Lee Ullery,

Superintendent of Construction,

U.S.Mint Building, Denver, Colo.

Dear Sir:-

We will put in place the conduits and wiring,as an extension of conduits and wiring under our contract, from near the foot of lamp standards at driveway entrance and to extend up to the top of said standards for lighting, the conduits and wire to be similar to that put in place under our contract for lighting said lamps, in the building under your charge, for the sum of TWENTY ONE DOLLARS ......($21.00).

(Signed) S.Faith & Co.,
S.

PRINTED HEADING.

Denver, Colo., May 3,1904.

Mr.Lee Ullery,

Superintendent of Construction, Mint, Denver.

I hereby propose to reduce contract price for finishing Mint Building Twenty two and .50 Dollars for omitting the putting in of four electric wire boxes near foot of the stone posts at Driveway entrances wire pipes handholes and so on more fully specified in paragrapg seven the latter half of same and also paragraph 8 and 9 on page 22 of the specifications.

Respectfully Submitted:

(Signed) James A.McGonigle,
By C.Anderson.

DENVER, NEW MINT.

99

OFFICE OF SUPERVISING ARCHITECT

IN REPLYING QUOTE UPPER INITIAL, RIGHT HAND CORNER

TREASURY DEPARTMENT F.B.W.

WASHINGTON May 4, 1904.

The Superintendent of Construction,

New Mint Building,

Denver, Colorado.

Sir:

The Office is in receipt of your letter of April 30th, relative to the ornamental plaster work over the corridor windows in the second story of the building of which you are the Superintendent of Construction.

In reply you are informed that, in view of the circumstances stated by you, if the work is carried out in accordance with the full size detail drawing No.159, same will be satisfactory to this office.

Respectfully,

J. K. Taylor
Supervising Architect.

M.

L

Custodian U. S. COURT HOUSE.

Santa Fe N.M, May 5 1904 . 189 .

Lee Ullery Esq; Supt/

Denver Colorado/

My Dear Mr Ullery;-

I have received the specifications for the repairs recommended by you on the above building. In a recent letter you said you would like me to give a friend of yours in Denver a chanee to bid on the brick sidewalk in front of the building. find on reading the instructions and specifications that the entire work must be let to one contractor and therefore it will be impossible to let that part of the work separate from the others. I inclose a copy of the Specification for your information and if you think you can get your friend to make a proposal for e work I will be very much obliged. On page I2 of said specification you will find this language:

COLOR SCHEME.

The walls of P O work room to be in buff &c.

As we have no P O work room in this building I do not know what the above means, will you please explain . Hoping you are in the enjoyment of good health and spirits I remain yours

Very respectfully

A. L. Morrison

Custodian.

DENVER, NEW MINT.

OFFICE OF SUPERVISING ARCHITECT

IN REPLYING, QUOTE UPPER INITIAL RIGHT HAND CORNER.

Inclosure 621.

TREASURY DEPARTMENT

101

WASHINGTON May 4, 1904.

Superintendent of Construction,
New Mint Building,
Denver, Colorado.

Sir:

I inclose herewith, for your information and the files of your office, a copy of Department letter of even date, accepting the proposal of S. Faith & Company, in amount eight hundred and fifty dollars ($850.00), as an addition to their contract for the mechanical equipment of the building in your charge, to install instruments made by the Weston Electrical Company, in lieu of those made by the Keystone Electrical Instrument Company.

You will note that of the above amount five hundred and thirty-five dollars ($535.00) will be paid from the appropriation for New Machinery, Denver Mint, under the control of the Director of the Mint, and three hundred and fifteen dollars ($315.00) from the appropriation for Mint Building, Denver, Colorado; and you are hereby authorized to certify and issue vouchers for payment on account of the work, as required by the terms of the contract and the printed "Instructions to Superintendents", and to present to the Disbursing Agent for payment those vouchers which are charged to the last named appropriation; and to forward to this Department (through the office of the Superintendent of the Mint, your City) those vouchers which are charged against

G.

the appropriation for New Machinery, Denver Mint.

A copy of the acceptance will be forwarded to the Superintendent of the Mint, your City, for his information.

Respectfully,

JSS

Supervising Architect.

May 4,1904.

Messrs. H. Faith & Co.,
#2427 Pennsylvania Avenue,
Philadelphia,Pa.

Gentlemen:

In accordance with the approval of this Department, your proposal, dated the 19th ultimo, as amended by your letter of the 22d ultimo, in amount eight hundred and fifty dollars ($850.00), is hereby accepted, as an [illegible] 9,1902 for the mechanical equipment of the new Mint Building at Denver,Colorado, to install instruments made by the Weston Electrical Company, in lieu of instruments made by the Keystone Electrical Instrument Company, a public exigency requiring this change in the work.

It is understood and agreed that this acceptance is not to affect the time for the completion of the work as required by the terms of your contract; that the same is without prejudice to any and all rights of the United States thereunder; and without prejudice, also, to any and all rights of the United States against the sureties on the bond executed for the faithful fulfillment of the contract.

Of this amount the sum of three hundred and fifteen dollars ($315) will be paid from the appropriation for Mint Building, Denver,Colorado, under the control of the Supervising Architect, and the sum of five hundred and thirty-five dollars ($535.00)

DENVER, NEW MINT, May 4, 1904, S. Faith & Co.---2.

from the appropriation for New Machinery, Denver Mint, under the control of the Director of the Mint.

Please acknowledge the receipt of this letter.

Respectfully,

Assistant Secretary.

1.
J.C.P.

MS

DENVER NEW MINT

OFFICE OF SUPERVISING ARCHITECT

IN REPLYING, QUOTE UPPER INITIAL, RIGHT HAND CORNER

102

TREASURY DEPARTMENT

WASHINGTON May 5,1904.

Superintendent of Construction,
New Mint,
Denver, Colorado.

Sir:

I have to acknowledge receipt of your letter of the 30th ultimo relative to certain marble columns at the building under your charge, which are too short, and you are directed to obtain a proposal for placing over the cap a square slab, each side to be of the same length as the diameter of the columns at neck, and forward such proposal to this Office with your definite recommendation.

Respectfully,

J. K. Taylor
Supervising Architect.

HM

DENVER MINT (new)

103

TREASURY DEPARTMENT FBW

OFFICE OF SUPERVISING ARCHITECT

IN REPLYING QUOTE UPPER INITIAL RIGHT HAND CORNER

(FORWARDING)

WASHINGTON May 5,1904.

The Superintendent of Construction,

New Mint Building,

Denver, Colorado.

Sir:

There have this day been forwarded for your information and files three photographs taken from approved models for certain ornamental work about the entrance to the building of which you are the Superintendent of Construction.

Respectfully,

Supervising Architect.

R.

CHEYENNE

OFFICE OF SUPERVISING ARCHITECT

IN REPLYING QUOTE UPPER INITIAL, RIGHT HAND CORNER.

102

TREASURY DEPARTMENT

WASHINGTON May 5,1904.

Superintendent of Construction,
New Mint,
Denver, Colorado.

Sir:

I have to acknowledge receipt of your letter of the 28th ultimo relative to the inspection of certain ornamental iron work for elevator inclosure at the Public Building, Cheyenne, Wyoming, and you are directed to prepare a sketch showing reinforcement of 1/2 x 3/16 wrought iron rings between rods of grilles, obtain a proposal based thereon and forward it to this Office with your definite recommendation, together with a copy of the said sketch, upon receipt of which prompt action will be taken. The stiffening to be applied only to panels where people come in contact with grille.

A copy of this letter has been forwarded to the Superintendent of the building, for his information.

Respectfully,

J K Taylor
Supervising Architect.

HM

DENVER MINT

M

OFFICE OF SUPERVISING ARCHITECT

IN REPLYING QUOTE UPPER INITIAL RIGHT HAND CORNER

Inclosure 721.

TREASURY DEPARTMENT

103

S

WASHINGTON May 5, 1904.

Superintendent of Construction,

U. S. Mint,

Denver, Colo.

Sir:

Referring to your communication of the 26th ultimo in relation to this matter, please find inclosed herewith a copy of Department letter this day addressed to the Citizens Alliance of Denver, Colo., regarding complaints made against your action in not permitting certain structural iron workers to work in the construction of floors for vaults in the building under your charge.

Respectfully,

L. [illegible]

J K Taylor
Supervising Architect.

DENVER MINT

In replying to this letter the initials in upper right-hand corner must be referred to.

TREASURY DEPARTMENT,

OFFICE OF THE SECRETARY.

Washington, May 5, 1904.

The Citizens' Alliance of Denver,

Chamber of Commerce,

Denver, Colo.

Gentlemen:

Your communication of the 16th ultimo was duly received with inclosures in relation to the alleged action of Mr. Lee Ullery, Superintendent of Construction, in charge of the U. S. Mint at Denver, Colo., in discriminating in favor of labor unions, and the complaints and charges made by you have been given due and fair consideration.

A uniform policy of this Department is not to interfere in matters between contractors and labor unions, it requiring only that the contractors shall comply fully with all the terms of their contracts with the United States.

From the facts in this case, as gathered from the statements submitted by you and from information secured from other sources, the Department is of the opinion that Superintendent Ullery's interpretation of the contracts in force at that building, as they were affected by the conditions which gave rise to your complaints, is entirely correct, and that his action was not in discrimination against either the Citizens' Alliance or the Structural Iron Workers' Union, but was based upon what in his judgment were his duties to secure the uninterrupted progress of the work as provided for in the contracts.

A copy of this letter will be sent to the Secretary of the Citizens' Industrial Association of America, at Dayton, Ohio.

Respectfully,

(Signed) H. A. Taylor

Acting Secretary.

S
T

DENVER MINT (NEW)

106

TREASURY DEPARTMENT

WASHINGTON May 7, 1904.

IN REPLYING QUOTE UPPER INITIAL, RIGHT HAND CORNER

Superintendent of Construction,
Mint Building, (New),
Denver, Col.

Sir:

Please forward to this office, in accordance with Section XXI, Paragraph 3, of "Instructions to Custodians, 1900," an account of sale of condemned Government property, for which a certificate of deposit, in the sum of Two hundred thirteen dollars ($213.00), was issued by the Cashier of The Denver National Bank, Denver, Col., on April 29, 1904.

Respectfully,

[signature]

Chief Executive Officer.

OC

107

PRINTED HEADING.

Kansas City, Mo., May, 11, 1904.

Mr. James A. McGonigle,

Denver, Colorado.

Dear Sir:-

We wrote you some time ago regarding double trim for double doors for the Mint building. The factory writes us that it will be impossible to use double trim on the inside of the double doors as the extension bolt that has been accepted by the Supervising Architect is a surface bolt, and will occupy the space on the rail, so that double trim cannot be used on the inside. We would be pleased to have you secure a ruling either from the Government superintendent or the Architect regarding what double trim will be required. If they will require double trim on the outside of doors, we should be pleased to be informed at the earliest possible date.

We find in making our estimate of trim for circular transoms over first story windows, that there has been a miscalculation made as we find that some windows have no transoms, and some have fixed transoms, and some require fast joint butts, catches and transom chains. If you will kindly inform us the number of transoms that are hinged, we shall greatly appreciate the information.

Yours truly,

(Signed) W.B. Richards,
V.P.

G. J. PIPER, President. W. E. PIPER, Secretary. ERNEST F. PIPER, Treasurer.

108

The Piper Bros. Co. BUILDERS

Office 220 W. Second St. Pueblo, Colo. P.O. Box 3.

Pueblo, Colorado, May 10, 1904.

Mr. Lee Ullerry,

Supt. United States Mint,

Denver, Colo.

Dear Sir:

Upon examining the plan submitted to us, by the Supervising architect of the U. S., for certain changes, which are contemplated in the Post office building of Pueblo, and upon which we intend to make a bid for the contract, we find some points upon which we wish some information.

First, we notice that an I beam column is planned to be placed immediately under a fifteen-inch I beam in the basement. We notice that there is a solid brick wall under this fifteen-inch I, and we wonder if the I beam column will still be needed.

Second, at the point marked X in the new lobby on the plan which we send you, we find a four-inch cast iron soil pipe and two water supply pipes extending into the upper stories. When the new screens are in place and screen L removed to M, these pipes will be exposed in the new lobby and, unless some provision is made, to conceal them or change their location, it will make a very unsightly feature. We presume, although we have made no careful examination, that these pipes might be moved.

Third, When screen L is removed to M, it seems to us that a new piece of marble wains-coating will be required at A, about two feet, six inches wide by ~~eight~~ 7 feet high. We are in doubt

109

OFFICE OF

Custodian U. S. COURT HOUSE.

Santa Fe N.M,May IO I904 18

Lee Ullery Esq

Supt of Construction.

Denver Colo.

Dear Mr Ullery:)

As you will notice by reading the specifications I sent youthe construction of the Gess Pool for blowing off the boiler into,is not included therein and we need the Pool very much I wish you would write to the Supervising Architect and have him authorise me to ask for bids to make the same.The Fireman says it must be at least 8 feet deep. As our heating season closes on the last day of the present month the work can be commenced immediately after that time.As you suggested I wrote to the Supervising Architect about the P O work room".

Very respectfully

[signature]

Custodian.

I wish you could spare us a little rain -we are actually drying up here.

DENVER, NEW MINT.

OFFICE OF SUPERVISING ARCHITECT

IN REPLYING QUOTE UPPER INITIAL RIGHT HAND CORNER

110

TREASURY DEPARTMENT

WASHINGTON May 11, 1904.

Inclosure No. 1826.

Superintendent of Construction,
New Mint Building,
Denver, Colo.

Sir:-

There is inclosed herewith, for your information and the files of your office, copy of Department letter of even date, accepting the proposal of S. Faith & Company, in amount twenty-one dollars ($21.00), as an addition to their contract for the mechanical equipment of the building in your charge, to put in the conduits, and wiring, etc., in connection with lamp standards at driveway entrance; and you are hereby authorized to certify and issue vouchers on account thereof, as required by the terms of the contract and in accordance with the printed "Instructions to Superintendents", payment of which vouchers the Disbursing Agent has this day been authorized to make from the appropriation for Mint Building, Denver, Colorado.

Respectfully,

J. K. Taylor
Supervising Architect.

KCH

May 11, 1904.

Messrs. S. Faith & Co.,
2427 Pennsylvania, Ave.,
Philadelphia, Pa.

Gentlemen:-

In view of the recommendation contained in letter of the 4th instant, from the Superintendent of Construction for the New Mint building, Denver, Colorado, your proposal of April 26, 1904, in amount twenty-one dollars ($21.00), is accepted, to put in place the conduits and wiring, etc., in connection with lamp standards at driveway entrance, as fully set forth in your proposal, the amount being deemed reasonable and a public exigency requiring the performance of the work, which is to be considered as an addition to your contract for the mechanical equipment of the building.

It is understood and agreed that this acceptance is not to affect the time for the completion of the work as required by the terms of your contract; that the same is without prejudice to any and all rights of the United States thereunder; and without prejudice, also, to an and all rights of the United States against the sureties on the bond executed for the faithful fulfillment of the contract.

Please promptly acknowledge the receipt of this letter, a copy of which is forwarded to the Superintendent.

Respectfully,

Acting Secretary.

T.
J.C.P.

DENVER, NEW MINT.

OFFICE OF SUPERVISING ARCHITECT

IN REPLYING QUOTE UPPER INITIAL RIGHT HAND CORNER

TREASURY DEPARTMENT

WASHINGTON May 12, 1904.

Inclosure No. 1831.

Superintendent of Construction,
New Mint Building,
Denver, Colo.

Sir:-

There is inclosed herewith, for your information and the files of your office, copy of Department letter of even date, accepting the proposal of James A. McGonigle, to deduct the sum of twenty-two dollars and fifty cents ($22.50), from his contract for the completion of the building in your charge, for omitting four electric wire boxes, etc., near front of stone posts at driveway entrance.

Respectfully,

J K Taylor
Supervising Architect.

KCH

Mr. James A. McGonigle,
New Mint Building,
Denver, Colorado.

Sir:-

In view of the recommendation contained in letter of the 4th instant, from the Superintendent of Construction for the New Mint building at Denver, Colorado, your proposal of May 3, 1904, to deduct the sum of twenty-two dollars and fifty cents ($22.50), from your contract for the completion of the building, for omitting four electric wire boxes, etc., near foot of stone posts at driveway entrance, as fully set forth in your above mentioned proposal, is accepted, the amount being deemed reasonable and a public exigency requiring the omission of this work.

It is understood and agreed that this acceptance is not to affect the time for the completion of the work as required by the terms of the contract; that the same is without prejudice to any and all rights of the United States thereunder, and without prejudice, also, to any and all rights of the United States against the sureties on the bond executed for the faithful fulfillment of the contract.

Please promptly acknowledge the receipt of this letter, a copy of which is forwarded to the Superintendent.

Respectfully,

Acting Secretary.

T.
J.C.P.
EC"

[illegible]

[illegible] Court House,

Santa Fe N.M., May 14 1914

Dear Mr. [illegible]:

I have just received a wire from the supervising [illegible] which says:

[illegible] to cost office work given in specification on courtyard can be [illegible] scheme can be used in court room if approved by you [illegible] what do you suggest [illegible] the title will be signed next Friday at [illegible] will be greatly obliged by a quick reply. When the work is finished [illegible] and the Secretary [illegible] you [illegible] in [illegible] place [illegible] my approval [illegible] have [illegible]

Truly your friend

[illegible]

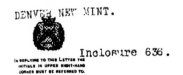

DENVER NEW MINT.

Inclosure 636.

IN REPLYING TO THIS LETTER THE INITIALS IN UPPER RIGHT-HAND CORNER MUST BE REFERRED TO.

113

TREASURY DEPARTMENT,

OFFICE OF THE SECRETARY,

Washington, May 14, 1904.

Superintendent of Construction,
New Mint Building,
Denver, Colorado.

Sir:

I inclose herewith, for your information and the files of your office, a copy of Department letter of the 13th instant, accepting the proposal of the Mitchell Vance Company of New York City, in amount seven thousand two hundred and forty-seven dollars and fifty cents ($7,247.50), for lighting fixtures for the building in your charge.

A copy of the formal contract, with bond, will be sent you as soon as executed by the contractors; and you are hereby authorized to certify and issue vouchers for the work, as required by the terms of the contract and the printed "Instructions to Superintendents", and to forward them to this Department, through the office of the Superintendent of the Mint, your City, for payment, charged against the appropriation for New Machinery, Denver Mint, under the control of the Director of the Mint.

File

Respectfully,

H A Taylor
Acting Secretary.

T.
J.C.P.
JSS

Forwarding.

May 13, 1904.

The Mitchell Vance Co.,
836 Broadway,
New York City.

Gentlemen.

In accordance with the approval of this Department, your proposal, dated April 28, 1904, addressed to the Supervising Architect, the lowest bid received, in aggregate amount seven thousand two hundred and forty-seven dollars and fifty cents ($7,247.50), is hereby accepted to furnish all the labor and materials required to furnish and place complete the lighting fixtures for the new Mint Building at Denver, Colorado, in accordance with the schedule in your proposal, as required by the specification dated March 31, 1904 and drawings numbered 100, 101, 102, 103, 107, 108, 109, 112, 115, 130, 200-A, EV-[illegible], EV-[illegible], EV-90, EV-91 and EV-92, and the drawings submitted by you, which have been given Department numbers 272, 273, 274, 275, 276, 277, 278, 279, 280, 281, 282, [illegible] and 284.

It is understood and agreed that the entire work is to be completed by July 1, 1904.

One set of the specification and Office drawings is forwarded herewith.

It is understood and agreed that you are required to execute a formal contract, with bond in the sum of three thousand six hundred dollars ($5,600.00), guaranteeing the faithful performance of the work, a form for which will be forwarded. This contract, with bond, must be executed in strict accordance with the rules printed at the head of said form, and be returned to the Supervising Architect of this Department at once.

You are further required to sign near the signature of the Supervising Architect the stamped set of said drawings, forwarded herewith under separate cover, and to return the same immediately for file in that Office as the contract drawings mentioned on the second page of that instrument.

The certified check which accompanied your proposal will be retained until the approval of your bond by the Secretary of the Treasury, of which you will be duly advised.

Payments for the work will be made as required by the terms of the contract from the appropriation for New Machinery, Denver Mint, under the control of the Director of the Mint.

Please acknowledge the receipt of this letter, a copy of which will be forwarded to the Superintendent of Construction of the building.

Respectfully,

Acting Secretary.

T.
J.C.P.

JAS

TREASURY DEPARTMENT.

Washington, D.C., May 16,1904.

The Supervising Architect,
Washington, D.C.

Sir:-

In the smoke chamber located in the Assayers work room,attic floor of the U.S.Mint building (new),Denver, Colorado, the top of cast iron stack extends within about two feet of the finished plaster line under roof of building. In the opinion of Mr.Healy,who is now at the building the heated fumes from furnaces below are liable to cause trouble,as they will have a direct impact against ceiling of chamber. To do away with this trouble it is recommended that the top section of pipe be removed, thus having top of pipe about on a level with the top of floor beams in attic floor,which position will allow gases to take a whirling action in chamber and be drawn direct through fan intake. No cutting is required to make this change, as top section of pipe,about four feet long, can be lifted off.

Mr.Ullery,the Superintendent of Construction at the building,mentioned to Mr.Healy that the shaft walls around stack might allow gases to enter rooms if the inside plaster cracked, as the bonding tiles had through holes at right angles to line of stack. No recommendation is made regarding this matter,other than the statement that if gases should enter working rooms it would be extremely unpleasant for the workmen therein.

Respectfully,
(Signed) R.E.Preston,
Acting Director of the Mint.

TREASURY DEPARTMENT,
Office of the Supervising Architect, May 17,1904.

Respectfully referred to the Superintendent of Construction for investigation and report and necessary action in the event the matters referred to herein can be attended to without action on the part of this office. T. F.B.W. L. C.E.K. (Signed) J.K.Taylor,
Supervising Architect.

NEW MINT BUILDING,DENVER,COLO.
May 21,1904.

Respectfully returned to the Supervising Architect with statement that smoke stack was constructed according to drawing No.125. Contractor will take off top section without expense to Government. Inner surface of shaft not plastered,not required by existing contracts except at top. Would cost nearly fifty dollars. Can be done later if found necessary,as Mr.Healy has asked contractor to construct manhole in north wall of shaft above attic floor.

(Signed) Lee Ullery,
Superintendent.

DENVER, NEW MINT

INCLOSURE 870

TREASURY DEPARTMENT

WASHINGTON May 13, 1904.

IN REPLYING, QUOTE UPPER INITIAL, RIGHT HAND CORNER.

115

Superintendent of Construction,
New Mint Building,
Denver, Colorado.

Sir:

This Office is in receipt of a letter from S. Faith & Company, dated the 5th instant, relative to elevator hoisting cables in the building under your charge, and a copy of the reply thereto, dated to-day, is inclosed herewith, for your information. You are directed to forward to this Office at once, 6" samples cut from each set of cables delivered at the building for use on elevators, marking each sample is such manner as to indicate for what elevator it is intended and what service it will perform on same.

Respectfully,

J. K. Taylor
Supervising Architect.

MM

Messrs. S. Faith & Company,
#2437 Pennsylvania Avenue,
Philadelphia, Pennsylvania.

Gentlemen:

I have to acknowledge receipt of your letter of the 5th instant relative to cables furnished by you on elevators at the new Mint building, Denver, Colorado, and you are requested to submit a proposal covering the use of steel cables of the weights given for the various classes of work in connection with the 20,000 lb. freight hoist, in lieu of Swedish iron cables of the sizes called for [redacted] tract for the mechanical equipment of the said building, upon receipt of which prompt action will be taken.

Respectfully,

Supervising Architect.

HM

DENVER, NEW MINT.

OFFICE OF SUPERVISING ARCHITECT

IN REPLYING QUOTE UPPER INITIAL, RIGHT HAND CORNER.

1160

TREASURY DEPARTMENT

WASHINGTON May 19, 1904.

Inclosure No. 1850.

Superintendent of Construction,
New Mint Building,
Denver, Colorado.

Sir:-

There is inclosed herewith, for your information and the files of your office, copy of letter of even date, rejecting samples marked as submitted by the contractor for the completion of the building in your charge.

Respectfully,

J K Taylor
Supervising Architect.

KCH

May 19, 1904.

Mr. James A. McGonigle,
New Mint Building,
Denver, Colorado.

Sir:-

There has been received in this Office, without letter of transmittal, a sample of varnish, brand Elastica No. 2, Finish, manufactured by the Standard Varnish Works, marked as coming from you for use in the New Mint building at Denver, Colorado, and you are advised that if this sample was submitted by you for use in the above mentioned building, it is rejected, inasmuch as the gums are low and it contains rosin and benzine.

There has also been received, under the same conditions, a sample of varnish, brand Pyramid Finish Interior, manufactured by the O'Brien Varnish Company, and it is rejected for the same reason.

Respectfully,

Supervising Architect.

May 23,1904.

The Supervising Architect,

Treasury Department, Washington, D.C.

Sir:-

I am informed by Mr.Healy(who is now at the U.S.Mint building(new),Denver, Colorado), that the positions of the coal holes in ceiling of coal storage vault, have been changed from positions as shown on the original drawings; the centers of the two covers now in place are about seven feet from back wall of vault. It is desired that coal be deposited in vault and stored without trimming over the entire storage space, and moving the inlets five feet back from center of room will limit storage space unless coal is rehandled.

It is recommended that two additional coal holes be provided to be installed on a line with and about 18 feet nearer building than the two holes now in place. As the brick arches are not in place at positions recommended, the only additional expense will be for the two casings with hinged covers.

Respectfully,

[illegible] of Construction,

U.S.S. 'New',

[illegible]

For your information [illegible] copy of [illegible] this [illegible], as [illegible] to the [illegible] Company [illegible] for the installation of [illegible] in the [illegible] for which you are Superintendent of Cons[illegible] of approval, [illegible] and marking.

A set of the approved samples will be forwarded [illegible] express, charges prepaid, and a set of fixture drawings [illegible] will be sent [illegible] day, if not [illegible].

Respectfully,

DENVER MINT (NEW).

MGD

May 24, 1904.

FORWARDING. (Mail and Exp.)

The Mitchell Vance Company,

#836 Broadway,

P

New York City.

Sirs:

Referring to your contract for furnishing lighting fixtures for the U. S. Mint (new), Denver, Col., receipt is acknowledged of your letter of the 20th instant, forwarding certain samples for consideration, and you are advised as follows:

The samples of tube, shells, and casing, showing finish, etc., are approved, and one set will be returned to you to-day, by express, charges prepaid, to serve as a guide. A similar set will be sent to the Superintendent at the building.

In view of the fact that the specification requires you to submit samples in triplicate, no action will be taken on the following until receipt of two more samples of each:

Wire, Nos. 14, 16, and 18, B. & S. Gauge;
McAllen Insulating Joint;
Pear Swithh;
Edison Key Socket;
Edison Keyless Socket;
Terminal Switch;
Insulating Ball Joint.

One set of building floor plans, drawings Nos. 100 to 108 inclusive, plumbing plan P-75, and drawings E.W.-88 F to E. W.-92-F, will be sent to you to-day, under separate cover. Drawing P-73 shows location of type M gas fixtures only.

Respectfully,

(Signed) J.K.Taylor

Supervising Architect.

L CEK

DENVER, NEW MINT.

118

TREASURY DEPARTMENT

OFFICE OF SUPERVISING ARCHITECT

IN REPLYING QUOTE UPPER INITIAL RIGHT HAND CORNER

WASHINGTON May 24, 1904.

Inclosure No. 1764.

Superintendent of Construction,
New Mint Building,
Denver, Colo.

Sir:-

There is inclosed herewith, for your information and the files of your office, copy of Department letter of even date, accepting the proposal of Messrs. S. Faith & Company, to substitute steel cables for the Swedish iron cables required by their contract for the mechanical equipment of the building in your charge, for the 20,000-pound freight hoist now being installed, without extra cost to the Government.

Respectfully,

J K Taylor
Supervising Architect.

L.

KCH

DENVER, NEW MINT.

May 24, 1904.

Messrs. S. Faith & Company,
2427 Pennsylvania Avenue,
Philadelphia, Pa.

Gentlemen:-

Your proposal of the 18th instant, to substitute steel cables for the Swedish iron cables required by your contract for the mechanical equipment of the New Mint building at Denver, Colorado, for the 20,000-pound freight hoist now being installed, without extra expense to the Government, is hereby accepted, a public exigency requiring this change in your contract.

It is understood and agreed that this acceptance is not to affect the time for the completion of the work as required by the terms of your contract; that the same is without prejudice to any and all rights of the United States thereunder; and without prejudice, also, to any and all rights of the United States against the sureties on the bond executed for the faithful fulfillment of the contract.

Please promptly acknowledge the receipt of this letter, a copy of which is forwarded to the Superintendent.

Respectfully,

Acting Secretary.

DENVER MINT (NEW).

MGD

119

TREASURY DEPARTMENT FBW

IN REPLYING, QUOTE UPPER INITIAL, RIGHT HAND CORNER.

WASHINGTON May 23, 1904.

ENCLOSURE 73.

The Superintendent of Construction,

U. S. Mint (New),

Denver, Col.

Sir:

For your information find herewith copy of office letter of this date, addressed to S. Faith and Company, contractors for mechanical equipment of the building for which you are Superintendent, advising them relative to switchboard grille work.

Please modify your copy of contractors' drawing numbered E.W.-268, so as to show 1/2" grille work above and at ends of switchboard, instead of 1" as shown.

Respectfully,

Supervising Architect.

DENVER MINT (NEW).

MOD

May 25, 1904.

Messrs. S. Faith and Company,

2427 Pennsylvania Avenue,

Philadelphia, Pa.

Sirs:

Referring to your contract for mechanical equipment of the U. S. Mint (new), Denver, Col., receipt is acknowledged of your letter of the 21st instant, relative to switchboard grille work.

In reply you are advised that office drawing E.W.-95 is correct in showing 1/2" grille work above and at the ends of switchboard. Your drawing (office number E.W.-263) on which this office marked the bars as being 1" wide has been modified to show 1/2" bars, in accordance with the contract drawing, and the Superintendent of Construction has been so advised.

Respectfully,

(Signed) J.K:Taylor

Supervising Architect.

L CEK

[illegible]

[illegible] Agent,

[illegible]

[illegible] Colorado [illegible] 23rd [illegible] [illegible] of work also postmaster [illegible] [illegible] in [illegible] operation [illegible] September [illegible] will be necessary [illegible] not available [illegible] answer

[illegible] Taylor

[illegible]

[illegible] Government rate

[illegible]

PRINTED HEADING.

Denver, Colo., %/24/1904.

Mr.L.Ullery,

Supt.New Mint Building,

Denver, Colorado.

Dear Sir:-

I propose to furnish and set in place complete two coal hole frames with solid covers hinged,2'-0" diameter,according to Drawing No. 239nfor the sum of eighty six dollars and twenty cents ($86.20).

(Signed) James A.McGonigle.

DENVER, NEW MINT.

OFFICE OF SUPERVISING ARCHITECT

IN REPLYING QUOTE UPPER INITIAL RIGHT HAND CORNER

122

TREASURY DEPARTMENT

WASHINGTON May 24, 1904.

Superintendent of Construction,
New Mint Building,
Denver, Colo.

Sir:-

I have to acknowledge receipt of your letter of the 17th instant, relative to the blackening of the plastered ceiling of first story corridor of the building in your charge, and you are directed to obtain a proposal from the contractor for a coat of water color which will entirely cover the discoloration and forward it to this Office with your definite recommendation, upon receipt of which prompt action will be taken.

Respectfully,

Supervising Architect.

KC

DENVER, NEW MINT.

OFFICE OF SUPERVISING ARCHITECT

IN REPLYING, QUOTE UPPER INITIAL RIGHT HAND CORNER

1203 JP

TREASURY DEPARTMENT

WASHINGTON May 25, 1904.

Superintendent of Construction,
New Mint Building,
Denver, Colorado.

Sir:

I have to acknowledge receipt of your letter of the 15th instant with inclosure, relative to certain hardware included under the contract for the completion of the building under your charge. Your suggestion that the trim as required by the contract can be placed, provided an escutcheon and knob of the same size as those on the swinging leaf are substituted for the small escutcheon and knob on the approved extension bolt, is approved, and if this arrangement can be placed without additional expense to the Government, it will be considered as filling the requirements of the contract, if not, you are directed to obtain a proposal for the amount the contractor will deduct for supplying a top and bottom bolt, with handles within easy reach, the knob and escutcheon to be placed on each side of standing leaf, and forward such proposal to this Office with your definite recommendation.

Your interpretation relative to transoms over first story, exterior windows, is correct.

Respectfully,

[signature]

L

Acting Supervising Architect.

HM

DENVER, COLO. NEW MINT.

Inclosure 393

124

TREASURY DEPARTMENT

WASHINGTON May 28, 1904.

IN REPLYING, QUOTE UPPER INITIAL RIGHT HAND CORNER

Superintendent of Construction,
New Mint Building,
Denver, Colorado.

Sir:

There is inclosed herewith, for your information, a copy of Department letter of even date accepting the proposal of Mr. James A. McGonigle to make certain changes in the excavation for sweep cellar in connection with the building under your charge, without expense to the Government, all as set forth in said letter of acceptance.

Respectfully,

Acting Supervising Architect.

HM

DENVER,COLO.NEW MINT

May 26,1904.

Mr. James A. McGonigle,
Leavenworth, Kansas.

Sir:

In view of the statement and recommendation contained in letter dated April 22,1904, from the Superintendent of Construction of the new Mint building at Denver, Colorado, your proposal, dated April 21,1904, addressed to him, is hereby accepted to make certain changes in the excavation for sweep cellar included under your contract for the completion of the building, without expense to the Government, it being under stood and agreed that the doors to be placed in driveway are to project four (4) feet from the wall and run six (6) feet along same, and to be heavily checkered on top; a public exigency requiring this change in your said contract.

It is understood and agreed that this change is not to affect the time for the completion of the work as required by the terms of your contract; that the same is without prejudice to any and all rights of the United States thereunder; and without prejudice, also, to any and all rights of the United States against the sureties on the bond executed for the faithful fulfillment of the contract.

Please promptly acknowledge receipt of this letter.

Respectfully,

Assistant Secretary.

T
JGP
[illegible]

PRINTED HEADING.

Denver, Colo., May 28,1904.

Mr. Lee Ullery,

Supt.Mint Building,

Denver, Colorado.

Dear Sir:-

Your letter of May 27th asking for proposal to clean ceiling of first story corridor,I will clean the ceiling as proposed in your letter of the 27th without any expense to Government.

Yours truly,

(Signed) James A.McGonigle.

Form No. 168.

THE WESTERN UNION TELEGRAPH COMPANY.

INCORPORATED

23,000 OFFICES IN AMERICA. CABLE SERVICE TO ALL THE WORLD.

This Company TRANSMITS and DELIVERS messages only on conditions limiting its liability, which have been assented to by the sender of the following message. Errors can be guarded against only by repeating a message back to the sending station for comparison, and the Company will not hold itself liable for errors or delays in transmission or delivery of Unrepeated Messages, beyond the amount of tolls paid thereon, nor in any case where the claim is not presented in writing within sixty days after the message is filed with the Company for transmission.
This is an UNREPEATED MESSAGE, and is delivered by request of the sender, under the conditions named above.
ROBERT C. CLOWRY, President and General Manager.

RECEIVED at 1114 to 1118 17th St., Denver, Colo. NEVER CLOSED.

202 CH NB V 21 Paid Govt.

Washington, D.C. May 31,-4.

Supt. Constr. New Mint,

Denver, Colo.

Samples of cable for lifts one two and three satisfactory

J.K.Taylor Supervising Architect.

1230 p.m.

1226

PRINTED HEADING.

Cheyenne, Wyoming, May 27th, 1904.

Mr. Lee Ullery,

Superintendent New Mint, Denver, Colo.

Sir:-

We will furnish material and put in place 1/2" x 3/16" wrought iron rings in the spacesbetween the 1/2" square bars of elevator grills, where people come in contact with same. Said rings to be secured with 1/8" wrought iron rivets let through the Grill bars countersunk and heads finished smooth, the finish of rings to corres pond with other finish of grill work in U.S. Public Building at Cheyenne, Wyoming, for the sum of Four Hundred and Sixty seven dollars ----- $467.00.

Respectfully,

(Signed) Forster and Smith

By Edward Smith surviving partner.

PRINTED HEADING.

Denver, Colo., 5/31/1904.

Mr. Lee Ullery,

Supt. New Mint Bldg.,

Denver, Colorado.

Dear Sir:-

I propose to furnish and set complete four marble slabs of suitable thickness and dimensions to finish the 4 marble columns on second floor at no additional cost to the Government, the dimensions of said slabs to be as you direct.

Yours truly,

(Signed) James A. McGonigle,
E.M

IN REPLYING, QUOTE UPPER INITIAL RIGHT HAND CORNER

SUPERVISING ARCHITECT

TREASURY DEPARTMENT

S

WASHINGTON May 27, 1904.

Superintendent of Construction,

New Mint,

Denver, Colo.

Sir:

Please submit a report to this office on the condition of the vault work in the building under your charge as embraced in the contract with the Diebold Safe & Lock Co., stating what materials have been delivered and whether you have knowledge of any other materials being in transit. Also state whether satisfactory progress is being made in setting materials in place.

The office recognizes that work in connection with vault doors is somewhat out of your line, and wishes to know whether you consider that you can secure the installation of the same in accordance with the drawings and specifications, or whether you will require the assistance of the Vault, Safe & Lock Expert. If you will need his assistance, it would be preferred not to send him to Denver until the work is nearing completion.

Respectfully,

[signature]

L Acting Supervising Architect.

Superintendent of Construction,
New Mint Building,
Denver, Colorado.

Sir:

There is inclosed herewith for your information and files of your office, a copy of letter of even date ari[illegible] warded in connection with the contract of Mr. James A. [illegible] for the completion of the building under your [illegible]

While the approved sample of varnish bears the brand "Treasury Department Architectural," it is possible that material bearing a different brand will be delivered on [illegible] site, as the Department has requested Pratt & Lambert to discontinue using brands and descriptions pointing to [illegible] in connection with buildings under the control of this [illegible] and if varnish is delivered bearing the brand "Public Buil[illegible] ing Varnish," it is to be considered as the same brand of material approved, and you are directed to forward samples of same to this Office as soon as possible, for identification.

Respectfully,

Acting Supervising Archi[illegible]

Bu

Mr. James A. McGonigle,
Leavenworth, Kansas.

Sir:

I have to acknowledge receipt of your letter of the 4th instant and under separate cover sample of varnish, made by Pratt & Lambert, submitted in connection with your contract for the completion of the new Mint building at Denver, Colorado, and you are advised that varnish, as represented by such sample, is approved for use in the work, and the Superintendent has been so advised and directed to forward to this Office for identification, samples taken from material delivered on the site.

The following telegram was sent you on the 25th instant which is hereby confirmed:

"Varnish made by Pratt & Lambert, submitted May fourth, Denver Mint, approved. Letter."

Respectfully,

Acting Supervising Architect.

C

Bm

DENVER MINT, NEW.

OFFICE OF SUPERVISING ARCHITECT

IN REPLYING, QUOTE UPPER INITIAL, RIGHT HAND CORNER.

(ENCLOSURE #1595)
FORWARDING.

131

TREASURY DEPARTMENT FOBW

WASHINGTON June 1, 1904.

The Superintendent of Construction,

U.S. Mint Building,

Denver, Colorado.

Sir:

There is enclosed herewith a copy of Office letter this day addressed to Mr. James A. McGonigle, and, under separate cover, the photograph of the cartouche therein referred to, which it is presumed shows the completed plaster ornament for the corner of ceiling to be supplied under the contract for the interior finish of the building for which you are the Superintendent of Construction.

The execution of this model is apparently inferior to the model furnished by the Government, and you are directed to examine same, and, should the work not be carried out in accordance with the model furnished by the Government, it should be rejected, and you will please notify the contractor accordingly.

Respectfully,

J K Taylor
Supervising Architect.

B.

DENVER MINT,NEW.

June 1, 1904.

Mr. James A. McGonigle,

U.S. Mint Building,

Denver, Colorado.

Sir:

In reply to your telegram of May 26th,relative to the plaster cartouche to be supplied under your contract for the interior finish of the new U.S. Mint Building at Denver,Colorado,you are informed that the photograph referred to has this day been forwarded to the Superintendent of Construction for action,it being impossible to decide whether the work shown thereby is satisfactory or not,as,from the appearance of the photograph,the work seems much more poorly executed than was [illegible]

Respectfully,

J. K. TAYLOR.

Supervising Architect.

B.

DENVER, NEW MINT

OFFICE OF SUPERVISING ARCHITECT

IN REPLYING, QUOTE UPPER INITIAL, RIGHT HAND CORNER

1 5 2

TREASURY DEPARTMENT

WASHINGTON May 31, 1904.

Superintendent of Construction,
New Mint Building,
Denver, Colorado.

Sir:

This Office is in receipt of a letter, dated the 27th instant, from the Acting Director of the U. S. Mint, in which he requests two additional coal holes in ceiling of coal storage vault, at the building under your charge, installed on a line with and about 18 feet nearer building than the two holes now in place, and you are directed to obtain a proposal for placing such coal holes and forward the proposal to this Office with your definite recommendation.

Respectfully,

J. K. Taylor
Supervising Architect.

L
Jaco

HM

IN REPLYING QUOTE UPPER INITIAL, RIGHT HAND CORNER

MGD

TREASURY DEPARTMENT FBW

WASHINGTON May 31, 1904.

ENCLOSURE 194C.
FORWARDING EXP.

The Superintendent of Construction,

U. S. Mint (New),

Denver, Col.

Sir:

For your information find herewith copy of office letter of this date, addressed to The Mitchell Vance Company, contractors for the installation of lighting fixtures in the building for which you are Superintendent, advising them relative to approval of certain samples, a set of which will be forwarded to you by express, charges prepaid.

Respectfully,

J K Taylor
Supervising Architect.

L
Jas

DENVER MINT (NEW).

MGD

May 31, 1904.

FORWARDING EXP.

The Mitchell Vance Company,

T 10th Ave., 24th and 25th Streets,

New York City.

Sirs:

Referring to your contract for the installation of lighting fixtures in the U. S. Mint (New), Denver, Col., and to your letter of the 27th instant, forwarding two additional sets of certain samples, as requested in office letter of the 24th, you are advised that the following are approved:

Wire, Nos. 14, 16, and 18, B. & S. Gouge;
Insulating Ball Joint;
McAllen Insulating Joint;
Edison Key Socket;
Edison Keyless Socket;
Terminal Switch, except as to Handle, which must be in harmony with the rest of the fixture

The sample pear switch is rejected, as it is constructed for 125 volt service, and should be for 250 volts. The sample (in triplicate) will be returned to you, and you are requested to submit new samples, for 250 volt service.

One set of the approved samples will be sent to you to-day by express, charges prepaid, and a similar set will be forwarded to the Superintendent of Construction at the building.

Respectfully,

(Signed) J.K. Taylor, Supervising Architect.

Washington, June [illegible]

Instructions.

That you will, at the last day of [illegible] advanced to take office, [illegible] the following information:

The point of advancement in each [illegible]

[illegible] equipments of [illegible]

[illegible]

[illegible], and the [illegible]

[illegible] you are to [illegible] the proper [illegible]

[illegible]

Respectfully,

[illegible]

DENVER, NEW MINT

1,3

Inclosure 1114 TREASURY DEPARTMENT

WASHINGTON June 6,1904.

Superintendent of Construction,
Mint Building,
Denver, Colorado.

Sir:

There is inclosed herewith, for your information, a copy of Department letter of even date accepting the proposal of Mr. James A. McGonigle to clean certain ceilings at the building under your charge, without expense to the Government, all as set forth in said letter of acceptance.

Respectfully,

J. K. Taylor
Supervising Architect.

KM

June 8, 1904.

Mr. James A. McGonigle,
New Mint Building,
Denver, Colorado.

Sir:

In view of the statement and recommendation contained in letter dated May 25, 1904, from the Superintendent of Construction of the new Mint building at Denver, Colorado, and [illegible], of the same date, addressed to him, [illegible] [illegible] and one coat of water color, which will entirely cover the discolorations, without expense [illegible], is hereby accepted, a public exigency requiring [illegible] of the work in connection with your contract [illegible] completion of the building.

It is understood and agreed that this acceptance is not to affect the time for the completion of the work as required by the terms of your contract, and [illegible] without prejudice to any and all rights of the United States thereunder, and without prejudice, also, to any and all rights of the United States against the sureties on the bond executed for the faithful fulfillment of the contract.

Please promptly acknowledge receipt of this letter.

Respectfully,

Assistant Secretary.

DENVER, NEW MINT

OFFICE OF SUPERVISING ARCHITECT

IN REPLYING QUOTE UPPER INITIAL, RIGHT HAND CORNER

Inclosure 1124

TREASURY DEPARTMENT

1307

WASHINGTON June 7, 1904.

Superintendent of Construction,
New Mint Building,
Denver, Colorado.

Sir:

There is inclosed herewith, for your information, a copy of Department letter of even date, accepting the proposal of Mr. James A. McGonigle to furnish and set complete four marble slabs to finish four columns on 2d floor of the building under your charge, without expense to the Government, the size of the slabs to be as stated in Office letter to you of the 5th ultimo, all as set forth in said letter of acceptance.

Respectfully,

J K Taylor
Supervising Architect.

HM

Mr. James A. McGonigle,
New Mint Building,
Denver, Colorado.

Sir:

Your proposal, dated May 31, 1904, addressed to the Superintendent of Construction of the new Mint building, Denver, Colorado, is hereby accepted to furnish and set complete, four (4) marble slabs of suitable thickness to finish four (4) marble columns on 2d floor of said building, without expense to the Government, a public exigency requiring the work to be done in connection with your contract for the completion of the building.

It is understood and agreed that this acceptance is not to affect the time for the completion of the work as required by the terms of the contract, that the same is without prejudice to any and all rights of the United States thereunder, and without prejudice, also, to any and all rights of the United States against the sureties on the bond executed for the faithful fulfillment of the contract.

Please promptly acknowledge receipt of this letter, a copy of which will be sent to the Superintendent.

Respectfully,

Acting Secretary.

F
JCP

DENVER, MINT.

OFFICE OF SUPERVISING ARCHITECT

IN REPLY REFER TO INITIALS IN UPPER RIGHT HAND CORNER

138 JP

TREASURY DEPARTMENT

WASHINGTON June 7, 1904.

INCLOSURE 1560.

Superintendent of Construction,
New Mint Building,
Denver, Colorado.

Sir:

There is inclosed herewith, for your information and the files of your office, copy of Department letter of even date accepting the proposal of S. Faith & Co. to substitute, without expense to the Government, the Rumsey centrifugal pump in lieu of the Smith Vaile pump in connection with their contract for the Mechanical Equipment for the building in your charge.

Respectfully,

L. Kask

J K Taylor
Supervising Architect.

DENVER, MINT.

June 7, [illegible].

Messrs. [illegible] & Co.,
[illegible] Pennsylvania Avenue,
Philadelphia, Pa.,

Gentlemen:

Your proposal of the [illegible] instant to substitute, without expense to the Government, the Rumsey centrifugal pump in lieu of the Smith Vaile pump in connection with your contract for the Mechanical Equipment for the U. S. Mint at Denver, Colorado, is hereby accepted, it being understood that the pump substituted is to fill in all respects the specification requirements, a public exigency necessitating such substitution.

It is understood and agreed that this acceptance is not to affect the time for the completion of the entire work as required by the terms of your contract; that the same is without prejudice to any and all rights of the United States Government and without prejudice, also to any and all rights of the United States against the sureties on the bond executed for the faithful fulfillment of the contract.

Please promptly acknowledge receipt of this letter a copy of which has been forwarded the Superintendent of Construction.

Respectfully,

Acting Secretary.

T.
J.C.P.

R

DENVER MINT (NEW).

MGD

OFFICE OF SUPERVISING ARCHITECT

IN REPLYING, QUOTE UPPER INITIAL, RIGHT HAND CORNER.

TREASURY DEPARTMENT 139 FBW

WASHINGTON June 6, 1904.

ENCLOSURE 1208.
FORWARDING.

The Superintendent of Construction,

U. S. Mint (New),

Denver, Col.

Sir:

For your information find herewith copy of office letter of this date, addressed to The Mitchell Vance Company, contractors for installation of lighting fixtures in the building for which you are Superintendent, advising them of approval of pendant switch, sample of which will be sent to you to-day, under separate cover.

Respectfully,

J K Taylor
Supervising Architect.

DENVER MINT (NEW).

MGD

June 6, 1904.

FORWARDING (Mail).

The Mitchell Vance Company,

836-838 Broadway,

P

New York City.

Sirs:

Referring to your contract for installation of lighting fixtures in the U. S. Mint (new), Denver, Col., receipt is acknowledged of your letter of the 2d instant, forwarding (in triplicate) sample pendant switch, 250 volt, which has been approved. One switch will be forwarded to you to-day, under separate cover.

Respectfully,

(Signed) J.K.Taylor

Supervising Architect.

L CEK

PRINTED HEADING.

Washington, June 3rd,1904.

The Supervising Architect,

Treasury Department.

Sir:-

The following paragraph is quoted from a letter received from the Providence Engineering Works,contractors for engine plant,relating to conditions at U.S.Mint Building (New), Denver, Colorado;- "Referring to the work we are doing in connection with the power plant at the Denver Mint, we would respectfully request that the driveway,through which we must remove material excavated from the engine room,and through which we must also bring in the material for the construction of the foundations, be cleared of the material now placed there, so that wagons may pass through without obstruction. "

The material mentioned above is mostly rubbish; the result of cleaning up rooms on second story of building and throwing material into back drive-way. Teams can enter at west gate and turn around in driveway,leaving by same gate. Work is now in progress on ten ton scale,located at east gate, but scale is expected to be completed so far as driveway is concerned in about ten days from this date.

Respectfully,

(Signed) R.E.Preston,

Acting Director of the Mint.

DENVER NEW MINT.
V.

OFFICE OF SUPERVISING ARCHITECT

IN REPLYING QUOTE UPPER INITIAL RIGHT HAND CORNER

1141

TREASURY DEPARTMENT

S

WASHINGTON June 4, 1904.

Enclosure 464.

Superintendent of Construction,
New Mint,
Denver, Colorado.

Sir:

There is transmitted herewith letter addressed to the office, under date of the 3rd instant, by the Acting Director of the Mint, in relation to certain conditions at the building under your charge, which it is claimed, have a tendency to delay the work of installing the Mint machinery. You are requested to require the contractor, responsible for the accumulated rubbish, to remove the same immediately, in order that any cause for complaint may no longer exist.

You are requested to return the enclosure, and at the same time to advise the office whether all work under its contracts can be entirely completed before July 31st next; also whether the installation of any machinery to be used in the minting, will affect the completion of any branch of the work under the office contracts. You will also state, based upon the conditions, whether it is probable that the occupation of the building will be prolonged for any period beyond the time when the office contracts will be entirely completed, by reason of the non-installation of any minting machinery.

Your report is desired somewhat in detail, in order that the office may be fully informed of all the conditions, and be prepared to properly answer any complaint which may be lodged as to delay in the occupation of the building.

Should it be your judgment, also, that the conditions under any of the office contracts are unsatisfactory in any particular, with a tendency to delay the completion of the work involved, this feature should be treated in your report, and such suggestions and recommendations in regard thereto, submitted, as the Government's interests would seem to demand.

Respectfully,

J K Taylor

Supervising Architect.

DENVER NEW MINT.

Inclosure 1068.

IN REPLYING, QUOTE UPPER INITIAL, RIGHT HAND CORNER

142

TREASURY DEPARTMENT

WASHINGTON June 9,1904.

Superintendent of Construction,
New Mint Building,
Denver,Colorado.

Sir:

I inclose herewith, for your information and the files of your office, a copy of Department letter of the 9th instant, accepting the proposal of James A.McGonigle, in amount eighty-six dollars and twenty cents ($86.20), to furnish and place two coal hole frames and covers over coal vault;and you are hereby authorized to certify and issue vouchers therefor,as an addition to his contract for the completion of the building in your charge, as required by the terms thereof and the printed "Instructions to Superintendents",payment of which vouchers the Disbursing Agent has been authorized to make from the appropriation for Mint Building,Denver,Colorado.

FAB.

Respectfully,

J K Taylor
Supervising Architect.

JSS

DENVER. NEW MINT.

June 9,1904.

Mr. James A. McGonigle,

Care of Superintendent of Construction,
New Mint Building,Denver,Colorado.

Sir:

In view of the statement and recommendation contained in letter of the 27th ultimo, from the Superintendent of Construction of the new Mint Building,Denver,Colorado,your proposal, dated the 24th ultimo, in amount eighty-six dollars and twenty cents ($86.20), is hereby accepted, as an addition to your contract for the completion of the building, to furnish and place two coal hole frames and covers over coal vault, in accordance with the terms of your proposal, and to the satisfaction of the Superintendent, a public exigency requiring the immediate performance of the work.

It is understood and agreed that this acceptance is not to affect the time for the completion of the work as required by the terms of your contract;that the same is without prejudice to any and all rights of the United States thereunder;and without prejudice,also, to any and all rights of the United States against the sureties on the bond executed for the faithful fulfillment of the contract.

Please acknowledge the receipt of this letter.

Respectfully,

T.
J.G.P.

Assistant Secretary.

JBR

[illegible] MINT [illegible]

[illegible]

[illegible]

[illegible]

U. S. Mint (New [illegible]

[illegible], [illegible]

Sir:

[illegible]

The [illegible]

Respectfully,

[illegible]

The Mitchell Vance Company,

P 836-838 Broadway,

New York City.

Sirs:

Referring to your contract for installation of lighting fixtures in the U. S. Mint (new), Denver, Col., receipt is acknowledged of your letter of the 8th instant, submitting sample of art glass #4-1/2, for use in type B fixture, and requesting certain information in regard to type A fixture.

In reply you are advised that the sample referred to is approved for type B fixture. Also, that the approved fixture drawings show the ball globe for type A fixture, which modifies the specified requirements in that particular.

Copy of this letter will be sent to the Superintendent of Construction at the building.

Respectfully,

(Signed) J.K.Taylor
Supervising Architect.

144

The United States Mint, Philadelphia
Heating Ventilating & Plumbing Installed by S. Faith & Co

S. Faith & Co.
Contractors
FOR
Steam & Hot Water Heating
Plumbing & Ventilating Apparatus

OFFICE . 2427-33 PENNSYLVANIA AVENUE.

The Witherspoon Building, Philadelphia
Plumbing Installed by S. Faith & Co

Country Work Promptly Attended To.

~~Philadelphia~~ Denver, Colo., June 16, 1904.

Mr. Lee Ullery,

Superintendent of Construction, Mint Building,

Denver, Colorado.

Sir:-

Replying to your letter of the 3rd ultimo requesting a deduction for certain second-hand cast iron pipe, cesspools, etc., which have been used in connection with our contract at the Mint Building, we have to state that we find that 30 feet of 8" cast iron pipe has been used for sleeves, and one 6" cleanout and two 3" cesspools have been re-used, for which we hereby agree to deduct the sum of THIRTY DOLLARS ($30.oo) from the amount of our contract.

Respectfully,

S. Faith & Co

Copy

Mr.Lee Ullery,

Superintendent of Construction,

Mint Building, Denver, Colorado.

Sir;-

Replying to your letter of the 3rd ultimo,in reference to connections for the economizer installed at the Mint Building under our contract,we have to state we will place suction hose and connections to centrifugal pump for cleaning the bottom of fresh water tank in lieu of making deduction for omitting to make connections so that either side of economizer can be used as specified; and connections have been made at economizer so that it can be used as a whole for either heating feed water or for heating house water for the building,as requested.

Respectfully,

SUPERINTENDENTS.
C.

IN REPLYING TO THIS LETTER THE INITIALS IN UPPER RIGHT-HAND CORNER MUST BE REFERRED TO.

TREASURY DEPARTMENT, 146

OFFICE OF THE SECRETARY, S

Washington, June 13, 1904.

Superintendent of Construction,

Mint Building,

Denver, Colorado.

Sir:

By reason of certain information which has come to the knowledge of this Department, you are notified

First: That it is contrary to the policy of this Department to permit any Superintendent of Construction to maintain an office as an Architect, or to advertise or hold himself out to the public as an Architect soliciting private work, and Superintendents must govern themselves accordingly.

Second: You are directed to report to this Department in writing, without delay, what private practice of any nature or description you may have charge of as Architect.

Third: You are requested also to state whether you are engaged in a private capacity for income as representing building materials or in any other direction of a related nature.

Fourth: This communication must be replied to without delay.

Respectfully,

H. A. Taylor

Acting Secretary.

The Superintendent of Construction,
Mint Building, (new),
Denver, Colorado.

Sir:

Referring to the statements made in your letter of the 1st instant in regard to Mr.D.Goldstein refusing to fulfill his agreement to purchase the old fence and flagging on the site of the building in your custody, Department letter of April 19th last, is hereby modified as far as it relates to these items, and in accordance with your recommendation in your letter above referred to you are now authorized to accept the following proposals, they being the next best bids you could obtain, the old materials to be removed at once from the premises. Copies of the proposals are herewith enclosed.

James Collier, old stone flagging,	$ 125.00
Hyman Lifshitz's, fence around site,	20.00

Please secure payment of the purchase money before removal of the old materials and deposit the proceeds of the sale in the nearest United States Depository to the credit of the Treasurer of the United States on account of "Proposals for old fence and stone flagging."

The certified check submitted with Mr. Goldstein's proposal of March 30, last, will be forfeited, the proceeds will be collected and deposited in the usual manner in such cases.

Respectfully,

H A Taylor

Acting Secretary.

S
T

EXTRACT COPY,

PROPOSAL FOR OFFICE BUILDING AND OTHER PROPERTY AT THE U.S. MINT BUILDING, DENVER, COLORADO.

Denver, Colo., March 28, 1904.

Superintendent of Construction,
Mint Building, Denver, Colorado.

Sir:-

----- hereby propose to pay for the U.S.property offered for sale, the following amounts:-

* * * * * *

For fence enclosing site,
Twenty dollars ($20.00)

* * * * * *

(Signature) Hyman Lifshitz,

Address, 1336 Evans St.,
Denver,Colo.

EXTRACT COPY.

PROPOSAL FOR OFFICE BUILDING AND OTHER PROPERTY AT THE U.S.
MINT BUILDING, DENVER, COLORADO.

Denver, Colo., March 30, 1904.

Superintendent ofCConstruction,
Mint Building, Denver, Colorado.

Sir:-

I hereby propose to pay for the U.S.property offered for sale, the following amounts:-

* * * * * *

For stone flagging. $125.00

* * * * * *

Signature, James Collier,

Address #83 So. Logan Ave.,

Denver, Colo.

148

Form No. 168.

THE WESTERN UNION TELEGRAPH COMPANY.

INCORPORATED

23,000 OFFICES IN AMERICA. CABLE SERVICE TO ALL THE WORLD.

RECEIVED at 1114 to 1118 17th St., Denver, Colo. NEVER CLOSED.

26A.OB.M. 23 paid Govt

K.Washington DC June 14th-1904

Supt Ullery

New Mint Denver,Colo.

ractors may be permitted to set boilers that have withstood hydrostatic test.

J.K.Taylor.Supervising Architect.

843am

Form No. 16..

THE WESTERN UNION TELEGRAPH COMPANY.

INCORPORATED

23,000 OFFICES IN AMERICA. CABLE SERVICE TO ALL THE WORLD.

RECEIVED at 1114 to 1118 17th St., Denver, Colo. NEVER CLOSED.

282.ch.2r.y. 28-paid. Govt.

Washington, DC,June, 16

superintendent New Mint Bldg,

Denver, Colo.

Consideration will be given to Proposal for Changing blow off valves when forwarded with your recommendation

C. E. Kemper Actg Supervising Architect

3o8-p

DENVER, NEW MINT.

Form 186.
Ed. 8-29-1901 1,000.

ADVISING SUPERINTENDENT OF REMITTANCE OF FUNDS.

149

Treasury Department,

OFFICE OF THE SUPERVISING ARCHITECT.

Washington, D. C., **June 16, 1904.**

Superintendent of Construction,

Mint Building, Denver, Colorado.

Sir:

Your Estimate of Funds required during the month of **June ----------- , 1904 , for the work under your charge has been received, and you are advised that a remittance of $ 35,000.00,** to the Disbursing Agent, has been requested.

Respectfully,

Jas. A. Wetmore
Acting Chief Executive Officer.

ACF